STEPS ■ ■ ■ ■ ■ ■ 3h
MATHEMATICS

Contents

The coloured blocks at the top of a page show you that the work is mainly about:

■ number   ■ algebra   ■ shape and space   ■ handling data   ■ measures

A box like this at the top of a page tells you what you will need. We expect that you will always have a ruler, pencil, eraser and colouring materials so they aren't shown in the boxes.

balance scales, rice, plastic bag

Bar charts

Work with a friend if you can.

Peter found the lengths of words on some pages of a book by counting letters.

Tally Chart

Number of letters	Tally	Total
1	卌	5
2	卌 ⦚⦚⦚	8
3	卌 卌 卌 ⦚⦚	17
4	卌 卌 卌 卌 卌 卌 卌	35
5	卌 卌 卌 卌 卌 卌 卌 卌 卌	45
6	卌 卌 卌 卌 卌 卌	30
7	卌 卌 卌 卌 卌 卌	30
8	卌 卌	10
over 8	卌 ⦚⦚⦚	8

Bar chart of lengths of words

(bar chart: x-axis "Number of letters in the words" labelled 1 2 3 4 5 6 7 8 over 8; y-axis "Number of words" labelled 0 to 45)

1   List the word lengths in order, most common first.

2   How many 5-letter words were there?

3   Choose a reading book. Make a tally chart **and** a bar chart of lengths of some words on a page. Use RM1 to help you draw the bar chart.

4   Write three ways in which your bar chart is different from Peter's.

This **pictogram** shows the different newspapers taken by the families of Avril's friends.

Title Newspapers taken by the families of my friends	
key 📖📖 stands for 4 families	
Sun	📖📖 📖📖 📖📖
Daily Telegraph	📖📖 📖
Daily Mail	📖📖 📖📖 📖
The Guardian	📖📖 ▭
Daily Mirror	📖📖 📖📖 📖📖 📖
The Times	▭
The Independent	📖
Daily Express	📖📖 📖▭

1 How many families do these symbols represent?

a 📖

b 📖

c 📖📖

2 Use the pictogram to answer these.

    a How many families take the *Daily Mirror*?
    b How many families take the *Sun*?
    c Which newspaper is taken by 5 families?
    d Which newspaper is taken by 10 families?

3 List the newspapers in order with the one taken by most families first.

4 Survey your friends about newspapers taken by their families. Tally the data. Use RM2 to draw a pictogram of the results.

CHALLENGE

Work out how many newspapers are taken altogether in Avril's survey.

Closed and open

large sheets of paper

Here are some **open figures** made with 3 straight lines.

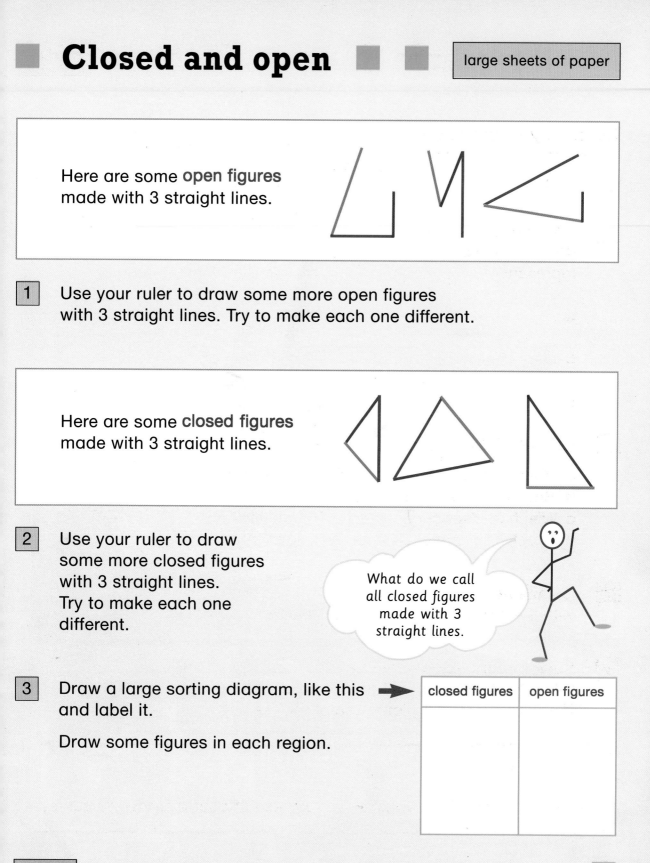

1 Use your ruler to draw some more open figures with 3 straight lines. Try to make each one different.

Here are some **closed figures** made with 3 straight lines.

2 Use your ruler to draw some more closed figures with 3 straight lines. Try to make each one different.

What do we call all closed figures made with 3 straight lines.

3 Draw a large sorting diagram, like this and label it.

Draw some figures in each region.

closed figures	open figures

All kinds of lines

1 Find examples of:
- vertical
- horizontal
- parallel
- diagonal lines.

Find patterns of lines and lines at right angles to each other.

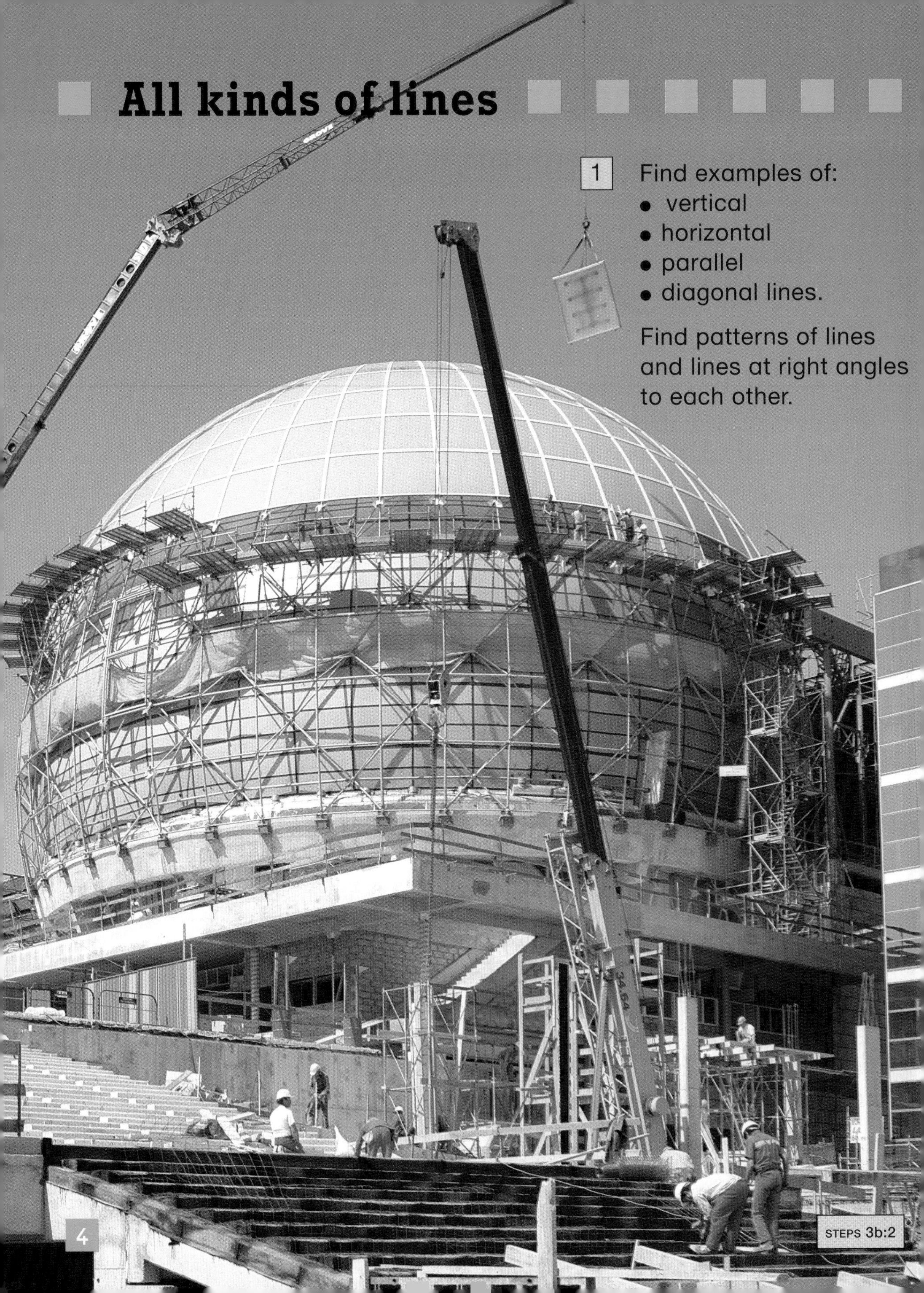

STEPS 3b:2

Multiplication

1 Copy and complete.

   a 5 × 2 = 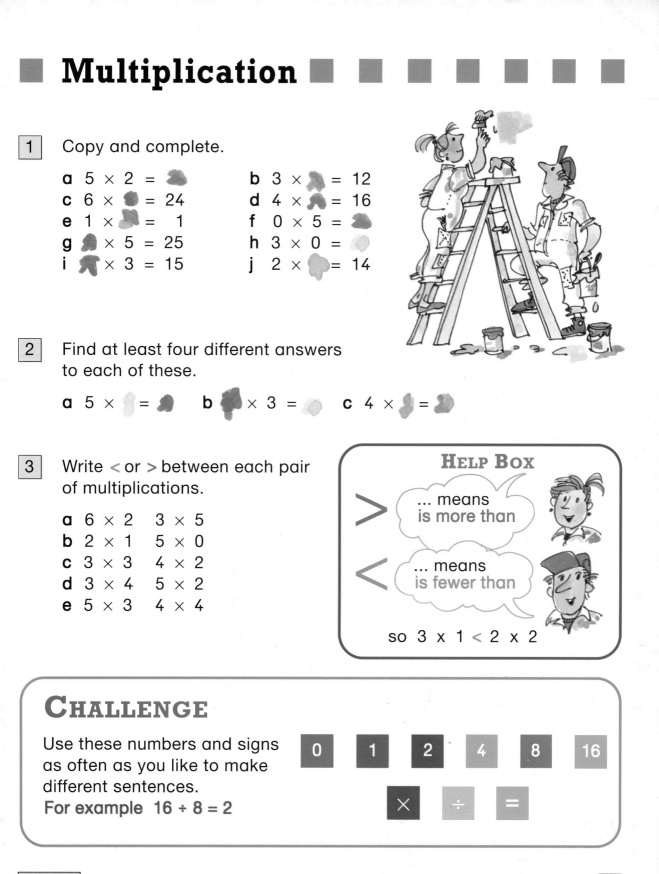   **b** 3 × ⬤ = 12
   c 6 × ⬤ = 24   **d** 4 × ⬤ = 16
   e 1 × ⬤ = 1   **f** 0 × 5 = ⬤
   g ⬤ × 5 = 25   **h** 3 × 0 = ⬤
   i ⬤ × 3 = 15   **j** 2 × ⬤ = 14

2 Find at least four different answers to each of these.

   a 5 × ⬤ = ⬤   **b** ⬤ × 3 = ⬤   **c** 4 × ⬤ = ⬤

3 Write < or > between each pair of multiplications.

   a 6 × 2   3 × 5
   b 2 × 1   5 × 0
   c 3 × 3   4 × 2
   d 3 × 4   5 × 2
   e 5 × 3   4 × 4

HELP BOX

> ... means is more than

< ... means is fewer than

so 3 × 1 < 2 × 2

CHALLENGE

Use these numbers and signs as often as you like to make different sentences.
For example 16 ÷ 8 = 2

| 0 | 1 | 2 | 4 | 8 | 16 |

× ÷ =

Team tables

1   Write down the numbers which are **not** in my team.

2   Write more numbers which are **not** in my team.

3   Write down the numbers which are **not** in my team.

4   Write more numbers which are **not** in my team.

5   Write down the numbers which are **not** in my team.

6   Write more numbers which are **not** in my team.

STEPS **3b:3**

Angles of turn

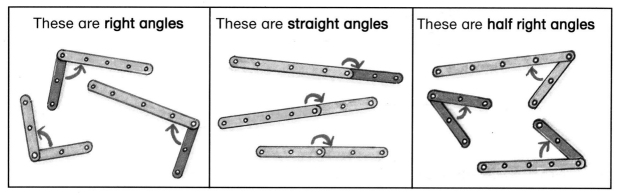

These are **right angles**	These are **straight angles**	These are **half right angles**

1 Copy this chart. Complete it by drawing the shape you will face when you have done the turns. Choose what to write or draw in the empty spaces.

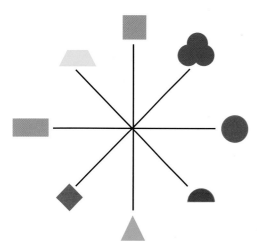

start facing	amount of turn	direction of turn	end facing
●	1 right angle	clockwise	▲
◆	1 half right angle	anticlockwise	
◗	1 straight angle	clockwise	
▱	3 right angles	anticlockwise	
♣	1 right angle		
▲		anticlockwise	
■			
▬			

2

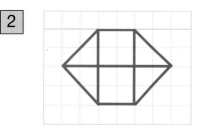

Draw this shape on squared paper.
Mark 4 half right angles in green.
Mark 2 right angles in blue.
Mark 2 straight angles in red.

Compass points

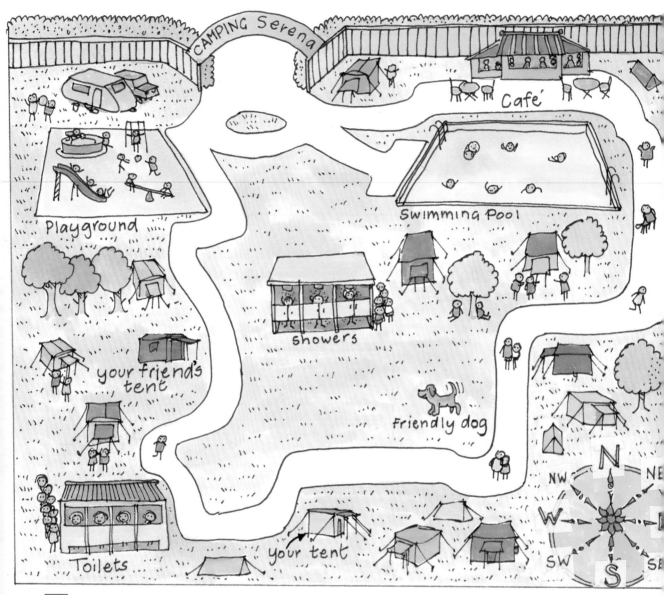

1 What is:

a North of the pool

b South of the showers

c East of the playground

d West of your tent

e North-East of your tent

f North-West of your tent

g South-West of the entrance

h South-East of the playground?

2 This compass has been turned.
In which direction are the aircraft moving?

a
b
c
d
e
f
g
h

3 This compass has been turned.
In which direction are the boats moving?

a
b
c
d
e
f
g
h

a.m. and p.m.

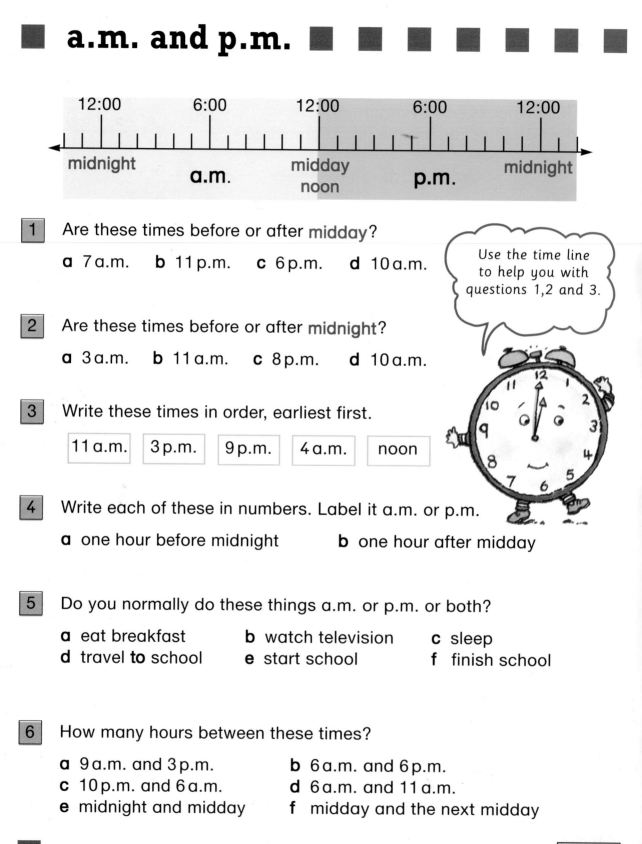

```
12:00          6:00          12:00          6:00          12:00
  |  |  |  |  |  |  |  |  |  |  |  |  |  |  |  |  |  |  |  |  |  |  |  |
midnight                    midday                        midnight
              a.m.          noon          p.m.
```

1 Are these times before or after **midday**?

    a 7 a.m.   **b** 11 p.m.   **c** 6 p.m.   **d** 10 a.m.

> Use the time line to help you with questions 1, 2 and 3.

2 Are these times before or after **midnight**?

    a 3 a.m.   **b** 11 a.m.   **c** 8 p.m.   **d** 10 a.m.

3 Write these times in order, earliest first.

    11 a.m.   3 p.m.   9 p.m.   4 a.m.   noon

4 Write each of these in numbers. Label it a.m. or p.m.

    a one hour before midnight   **b** one hour after midday

5 Do you normally do these things a.m. or p.m. or both?

    a eat breakfast   **b** watch television   **c** sleep
    d travel **to** school   **e** start school   **f** finish school

6 How many hours between these times?

    a 9 a.m. and 3 p.m.   **b** 6 a.m. and 6 p.m.
    c 10 p.m. and 6 a.m.   **d** 6 a.m. and 11 a.m.
    e midnight and midday   **f** midday and the next midday

Analogue times

■ ■ ■ | analogue clock face

1 | Write each time in words.

o'clock
5 minutes past
10 minutes past
15 minutes past (quarter past)
20 minutes past
25 minutes past
half past

a b c d e

2 | Write each time in words.

o'clock
5 minutes to
10 minutes to
15 minutes to (quarter to)
20 minutes to
25 minutes to

a b c d e

3 | This clock shows it is now 8.21. What time was it:

a 2 hours ago
b 15 minutes ago
c half an hour ago?

4 | What time will it be on the same clock in:

a 2 hours   b 25 minutes   c half an hour?

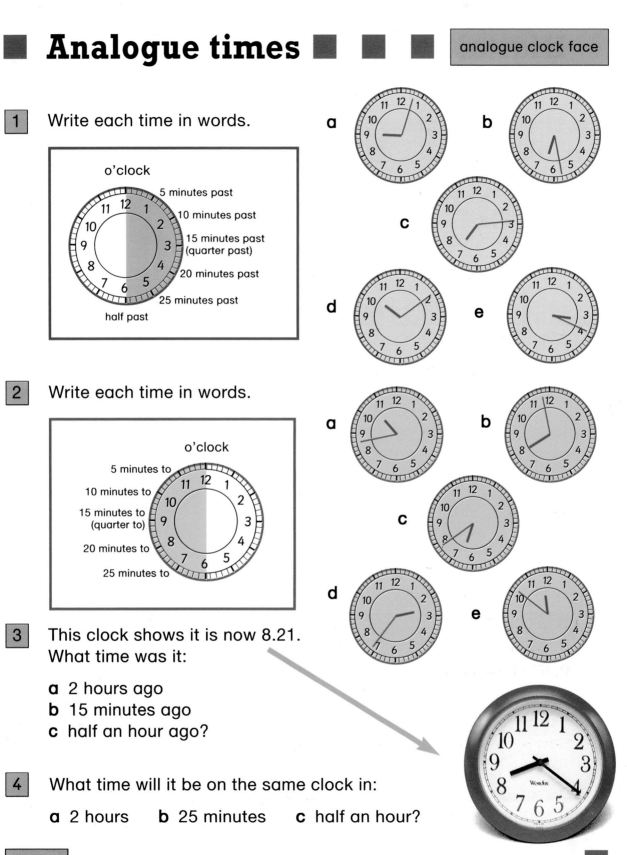

Digital times

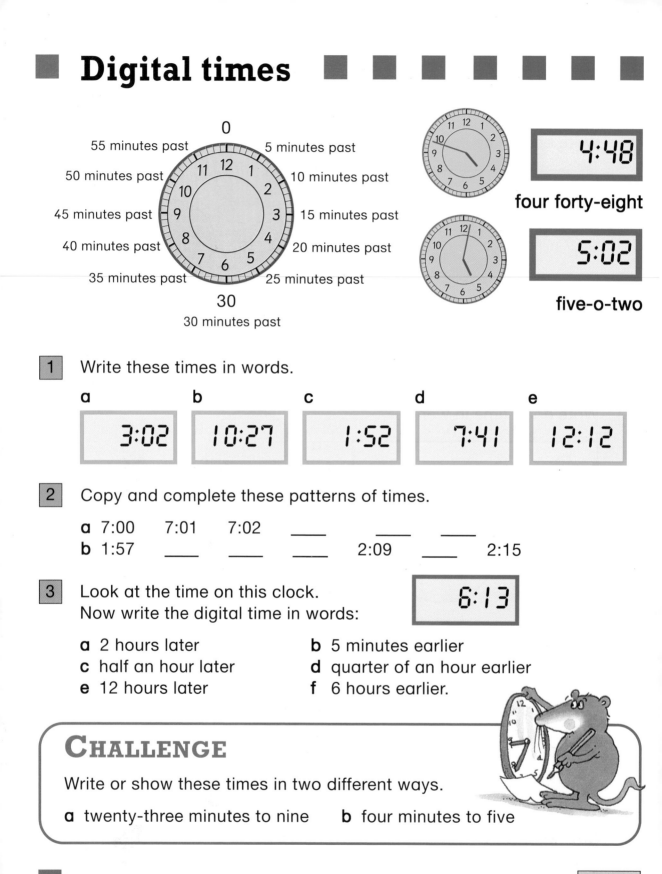

1 Write these times in words.

a 3:02
b 10:27
c 1:52
d 7:41
e 12:12

2 Copy and complete these patterns of times.

a 7:00   7:01   7:02   ____   ____   ____
b 1:57   ____   ____   ____   2:09   ____   2:15

3 Look at the time on this clock.
Now write the digital time in words:

6:13

a 2 hours later
b 5 minutes earlier
c half an hour later
d quarter of an hour earlier
e 12 hours later
f 6 hours earlier.

CHALLENGE

Write or show these times in two different ways.

a twenty-three minutes to nine
b four minutes to five

Adding with exchange

place value boards, base 10 materials

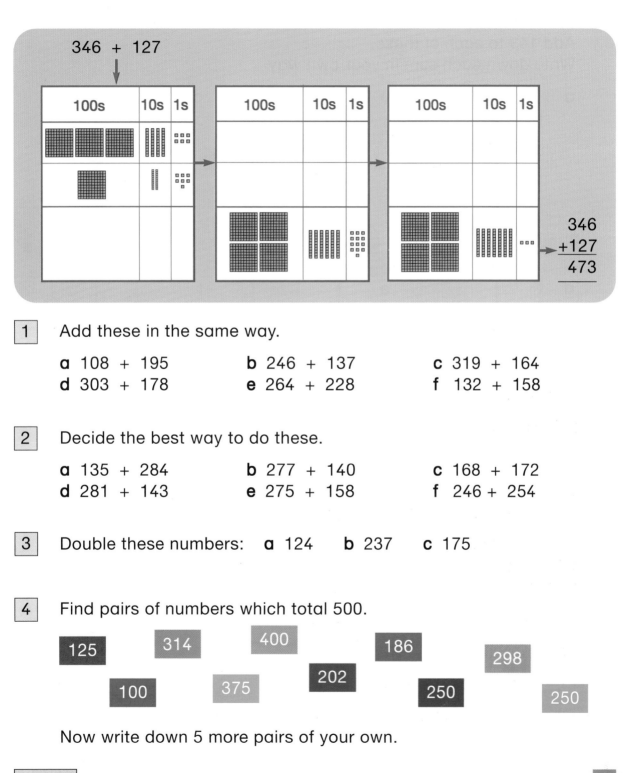

346 + 127

346
+127
―――
473

---

1 Add these in the same way.

a 108 + 195   b 246 + 137   c 319 + 164
d 303 + 178   e 264 + 228   f 132 + 158

2 Decide the best way to do these.

a 135 + 284   b 277 + 140   c 168 + 172
d 281 + 143   e 275 + 158   f 246 + 254

3 Double these numbers: a 124   b 237   c 175

4 Find pairs of numbers which total 500.

125   314   400   186   298

100   375   202   250   250

Now write down 5 more pairs of your own.

■ More adding ■ ■ ■

abacus and beads,
5 small blank cards

1 Add 143 to each of these.
Write down each sum in your own way.

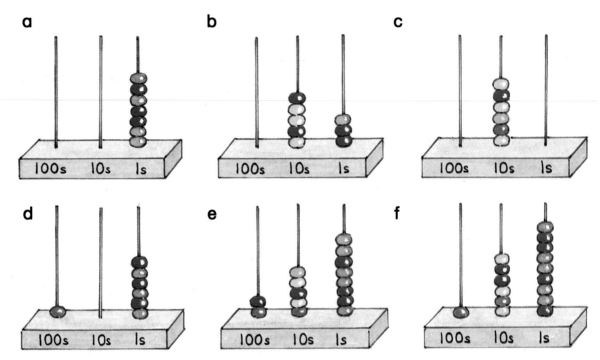

a   b   c

100s 10s 1s   100s 10s 1s   100s 10s 1s

d   e   f

100s 10s 1s   100s 10s 1s   100s 10s 1s

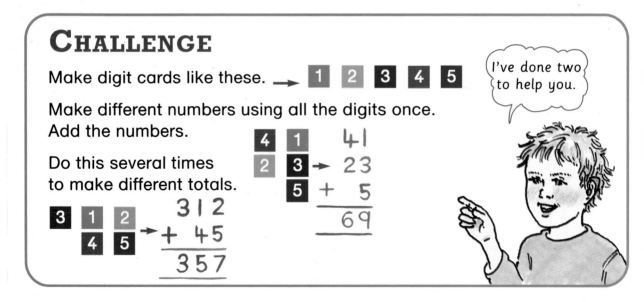

CHALLENGE

Make digit cards like these. → **1** **2** **3** **4** **5**

Make different numbers using all the digits once.
Add the numbers.

Do this several times
to make different totals.

4 **1**   41
2 **3** → 23
5   + 5
          69

*I've done two
to help you.*

3 **1** **2**   312
4 **5** → + 45
            357

Addition problems

Solve these problems in any way you like.
Write down how you worked out the answers.

1 Miss Adams works at the Post Office. On her busiest day
she sold 227 first class stamps and 185 second class stamps.
How many stamps did she sell altogether?

2 Ms Simms, the car park attendant, sold 123 parking tickets
on Monday. On Tuesday she sold 10 more tickets than
on Monday. How many tickets did she sell altogether
on the two days?

3 Mr Bell, in the fruit shop, bought two boxes of oranges,
each with the same number inside.
Altogether, there were 186. How many in each box?

CHALLENGE

On Tuesday and Wednesday, Mr and Mrs Lee
sold 96 comics altogether. They sold ten more
on Tuesday than on Wednesday.
How many comics did they sell:
a on Tuesday? **b** on Wednesday?

Ways to add

This is one way to add without using apparatus.

234 + 163

234 → 200 + 30 + 4
+ 163 → 100 + 60 + 3
300 + 90 + 7 → **397**

1 Write these in the same way.

a 236 + 253   b 182 + 217   c 130 + 318

d 464 + 32   e 343 + 156   f 267 + 121

2 Check your answers with a calculator.

This is another way.

234 + 163

```
  234
+ 163
    7   (4+3)
   90   (30+60)
  300   (200+100)
  397
```

3 Write these in the same way.

a 103 + 345   b 146 + 253
c 218 + 270   d 309 + 150
e 241 + 258   f 181 + 317

4 Do these in any way you like.

a 347 + 52   b 235 + 30
c 144 + 254   d 304 + 85
e 109 + 190   f 72 + 413

Double and halve

A3 paper, red, blue and green pencils

1 Try this.

On your paper, rule a red line less than 15 cm long.

_____ **6 cm**

Underneath the red line, rule a blue line twice as long as the red line.

Underneath the blue line, rule a green line half as long as the blue line.

Do this lots of times, starting with red lines of different lengths.

2 Afterwards, complete this sentence.

When you double and then halve a length ...

CHALLENGE

Design more pairs of loops like these.

Put different numbers in the blue circles each time. Keep the red boxes the same.

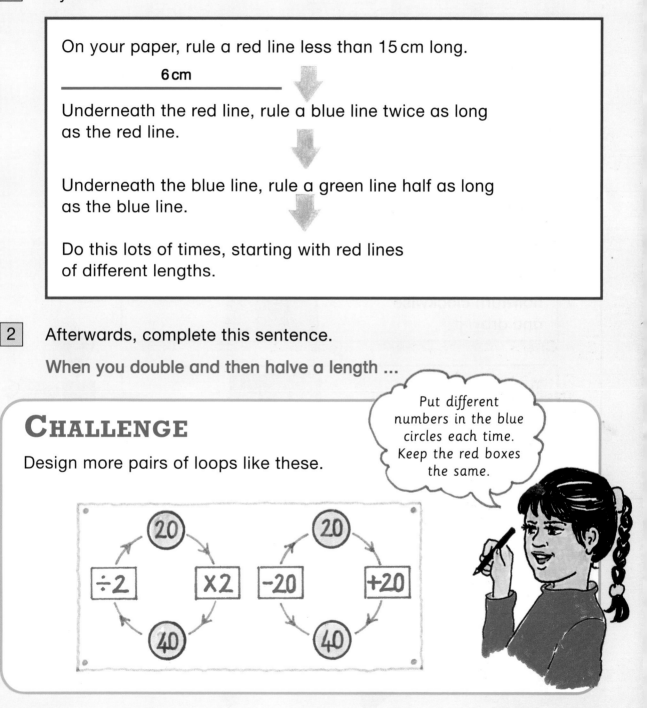

Back to the start!

Polydron or Clixi tiles, colouring materials to match

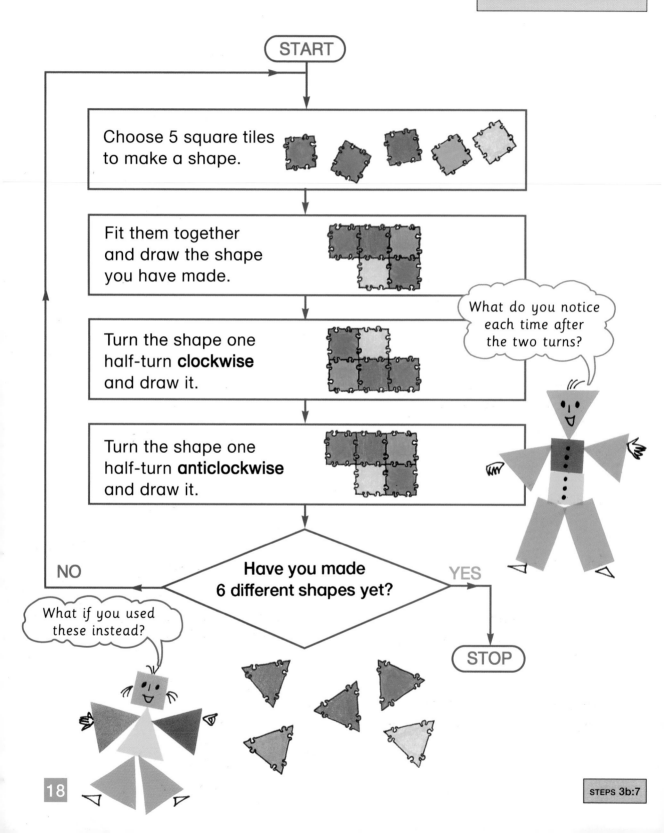

START

Choose 5 square tiles to make a shape.

Fit them together and draw the shape you have made.

Turn the shape one half-turn **clockwise** and draw it.

What do you notice each time after the two turns?

Turn the shape one half-turn **anticlockwise** and draw it.

NO

Have you made 6 different shapes yet?

YES

What if you used these instead?

STOP

18

Division

Grouping

Diana and her friends each took 2 biscuits from a packet of 15.

7 friends got 2 biscuits each with 1 left over.

15 ÷ 2 = 7 remainder 1

Sharing

Steve shared a packet of 15 biscuits between 2 plates.

Each plate had 7 biscuits with 1 left over.

15 ÷ 2 = 7 remainder 1

1 Find the answers by grouping.

a 12 ÷ 3 **b** 14 ÷ 4

c 21 ÷ 5 **d** 20 ÷ 2

2 Find the answers by sharing.

a 11 ÷ 2 **b** 18 ÷ 4

c 16 ÷ 3 **d** 19 ÷ 5

3 Divide one blue number by one red number each time.

13   25   17   20   **2   3   4   5**

Make as many different division sentences as you can.

Try to do these divisions in your head first.

Mystery numbers

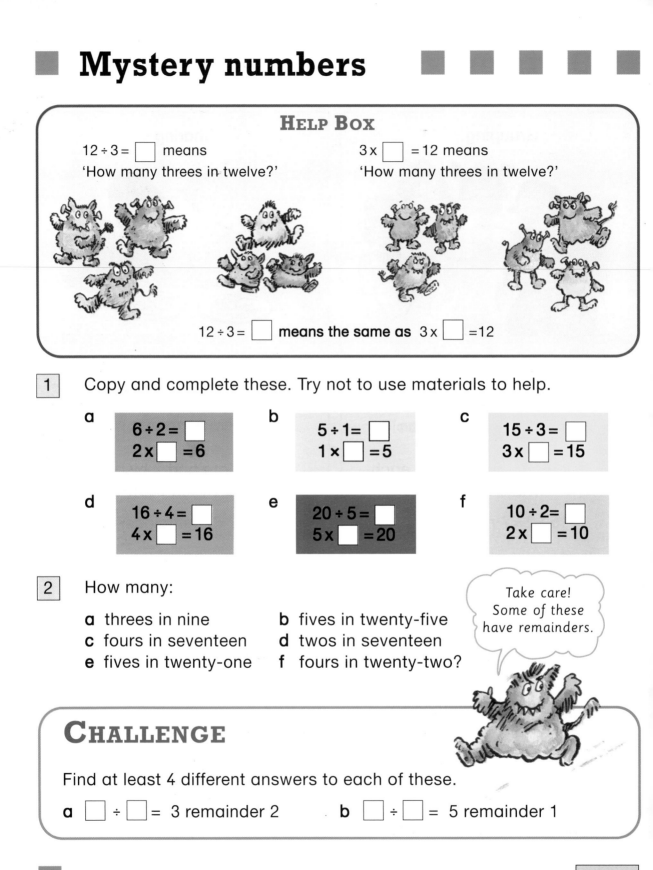

HELP BOX

$12 \div 3 = \square$ means
'How many threes in twelve?'

$3 \times \square = 12$ means
'How many threes in twelve?'

$12 \div 3 = \square$ **means the same as** $3 \times \square = 12$

1 Copy and complete these. Try not to use materials to help.

a
$6 \div 2 = \square$
$2 \times \square = 6$

b
$5 \div 1 = \square$
$1 \times \square = 5$

c
$15 \div 3 = \square$
$3 \times \square = 15$

d
$16 \div 4 = \square$
$4 \times \square = 16$

e
$20 \div 5 = \square$
$5 \times \square = 20$

f
$10 \div 2 = \square$
$2 \times \square = 10$

2 How many:

a threes in nine
c fours in seventeen
e fives in twenty-one

b fives in twenty-five
d twos in seventeen
f fours in twenty-two?

Take care! Some of these have remainders.

CHALLENGE

Find at least 4 different answers to each of these.

a $\square \div \square = 3$ remainder 2

b $\square \div \square = 5$ remainder 1

Rod lengths

1 Get one each of these rods.

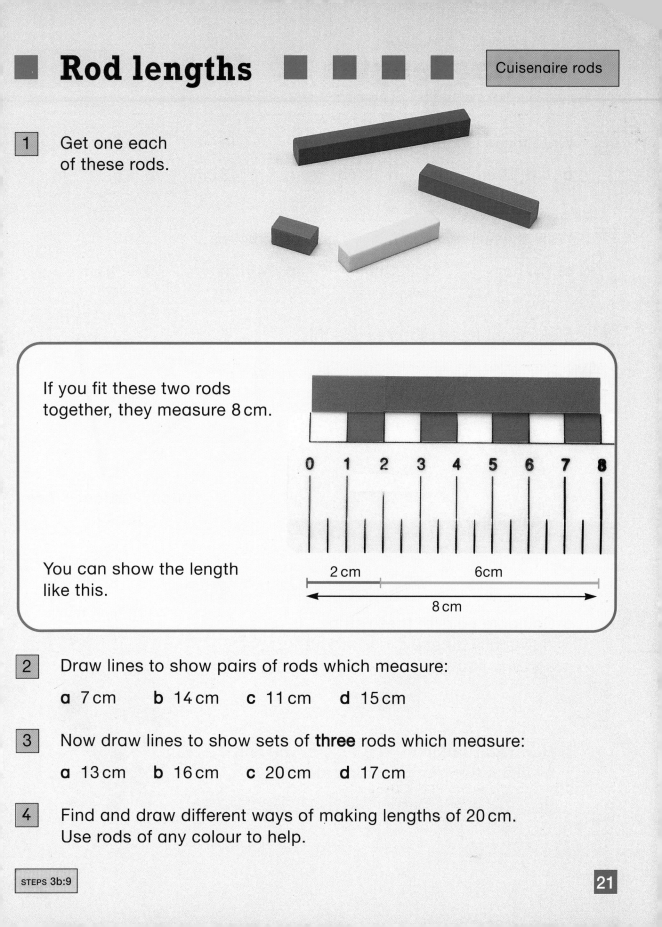

If you fit these two rods together, they measure 8 cm.

You can show the length like this.

2 cm   6 cm

8 cm

2 Draw lines to show pairs of rods which measure:

a 7 cm   **b** 14 cm   **c** 11 cm   **d** 15 cm

3 Now draw lines to show sets of **three** rods which measure:

a 13 cm   **b** 16 cm   **c** 20 cm   **d** 17 cm

4 Find and draw different ways of making lengths of 20 cm. Use rods of any colour to help.

Writing lengths

1 Write these lengths in centimetres.

   a 1 m 10 cm   **b** 4 m 83 cm   **c** 8 m 43 cm   **d** 9 m 27 cm

2 Write these lengths in metres and centimetres.

   a 187 cm   **b** 220 cm   **c** 746 cm   **d** 309 cm

3 Make eight more triangles like this.

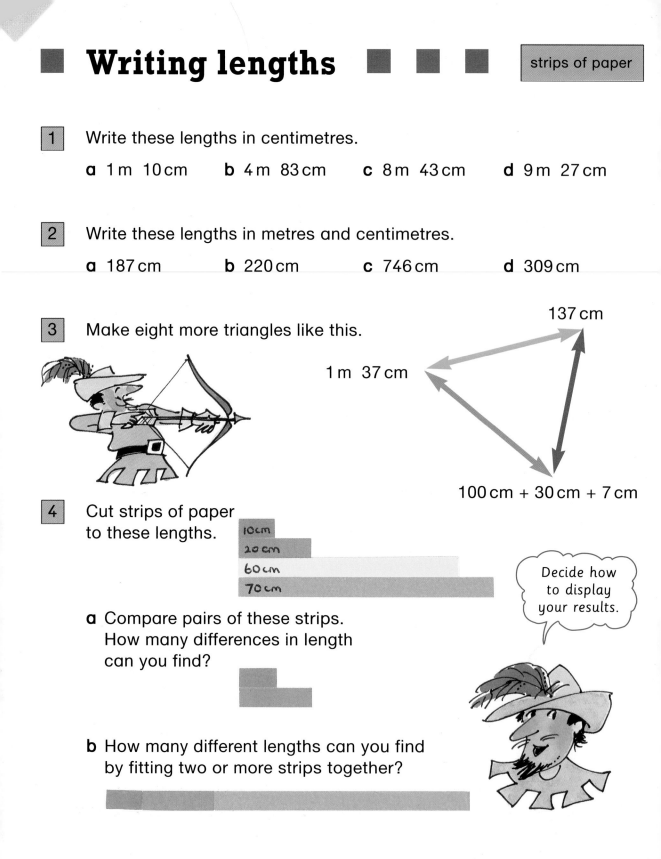

137 cm

1 m 37 cm

100 cm + 30 cm + 7 cm

4 Cut strips of paper to these lengths.

10 cm
20 cm
60 cm
70 cm

Decide how to display your results.

a Compare pairs of these strips. How many differences in length can you find?

b How many different lengths can you find by fitting two or more strips together?

22

Length problems ■ ■ ■ ■ ■

Try to work out the answers in your head first,
even if you choose materials to help you.

1   Harry is 97 cm tall.
His Dad is twice as tall.
What height is his Dad?

2   Pam's mum says she is
36 cm taller than Pam.
If Mum is 154 cm tall,
what height is Pam?

3   The kitchen table is square. Each side of the table-top
is 60 cm long. What is its perimeter?

4   Mum bought 1·6 m of red ribbon for Pam's hair.
Pam cut it into four equal lengths.
How long is each piece of ribbon?

5   Harry explained, 'The swimming pool is 0·9 m
at the shallow end and 3·3 m at the deep end.'
How much deeper is it
at the deep end?

CHALLENGE

Show how you work out the answer.

Pam said, 'I can swim thirteen lengths of the pool without stopping.'
Each length of the pool is 25 m. **How far can Pam swim without stopping?**

Place values

1 Write in figures:

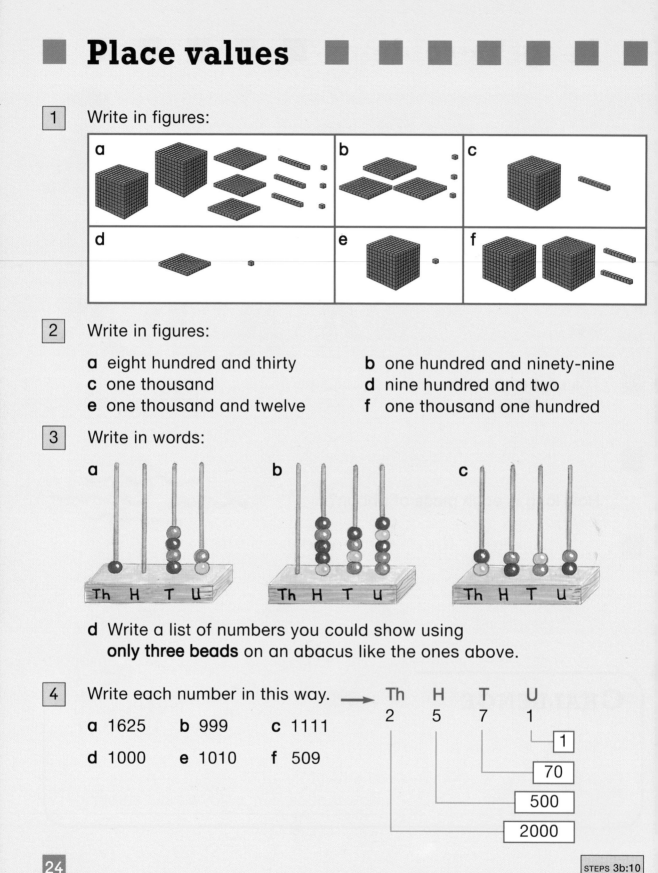

2 Write in figures:

a eight hundred and thirty
c one thousand
e one thousand and twelve

b one hundred and ninety-nine
d nine hundred and two
f one thousand one hundred

3 Write in words:

a

b

c

Th H T U

Th H T U

Th H T U

d Write a list of numbers you could show using
only three beads on an abacus like the ones above.

4 Write each number in this way. ⟶

Th	H	T	U
2	5	7	1

a 1625   b 999   c 1111

d 1000   e 1010   f 509

1
70
500
2000

Comparing numbers

1 Copy the pairs of numbers. Write the correct symbol, > or <, between each pair.

a $\boxed{1111.}$ $\boxed{1101.}$

b $\boxed{1876.}$ $\boxed{1786.}$

c $\boxed{1232.}$ $\boxed{1223.}$

d $\boxed{1776.}$ $\boxed{1767.}$

REMEMBER

2 Write the number **1 more** than:

a 1427   b 1010   c 1101   d 1300.

3 Write the number **10 less** than:

a 1777   b 1234   c 1010   d 1000.

4 Write the number **100 more** than:

a 900   b 1325   c 1077   d 1566.

5 Write the number **1000 less** than:

a 1547   b 1999   c 1000   d 1010.

6 Write these numbers in order of size, largest first.

a 1011   929   992   1101   1320   1232

b 1092   1200   1000   1029   1220   1209

Rounding

■ ■ ■ ■ ■ ■ ■ ■

```
0    100   200   300   400   500   600   700   800   900   1000  1100
|     |     |     |     |     |     |     |     |     |     |     |
   50    150   250   350   450   550   650   750   850   950   1000
```

1 Write these numbers to the nearest 100.

　a 122　　**b** 777　　**c** 834　　**d** 961　　**e** 1040

　f 39　　**g** 1075　　**h** 450　　**i** 950　　**j** 1001

2 Copy and complete.

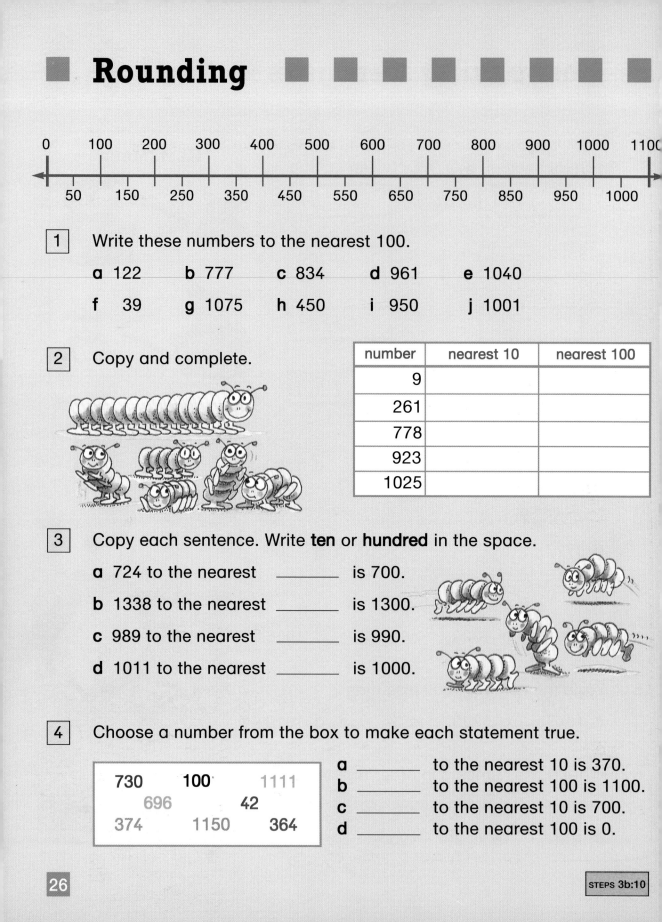

number	nearest 10	nearest 100
9		
261		
778		
923		
1025		

3 Copy each sentence. Write **ten** or **hundred** in the space.

　a 724 to the nearest _____ is 700.

　b 1338 to the nearest _____ is 1300.

　c 989 to the nearest _____ is 990.

　d 1011 to the nearest _____ is 1000.

4 Choose a number from the box to make each statement true.

730	100	1111
696		42
374	1150	364

　a _____ to the nearest 10 is 370.
　b _____ to the nearest 100 is 1100.
　c _____ to the nearest 10 is 700.
　d _____ to the nearest 100 is 0.

26

A ten for 10 ones

baseboard,
base 10 materials

HELP BOX

This is **one** way to find the answers.

245 − 118

100s	10s	1s

You haven't enough ones to take away 8 so exchange a ten for 10 ones.

100s	10s	1s

Now you can take away 118.

100s	10s	1s

127 left

245 − 118 = 127

---

1 Work out the answers.

a 145 - 127   **b** 253 - 138
c 274 - 146   **d** 382 - 167

e 482   **f** 320
    − 59   −113
    ‾‾‾‾   ‾‾‾‾

g 234   **h** 470
    −105   − 48
    ‾‾‾‾   ‾‾‾‾

2 Subtract 137 from each of these.

a 273   **b** 185   **c** 341
d 450   **e** 244   **f** 444

3 At Hill School there are 391 children.

a 236 stay for dinner. How many go home?

b There are 195 girls. How many boys are there?

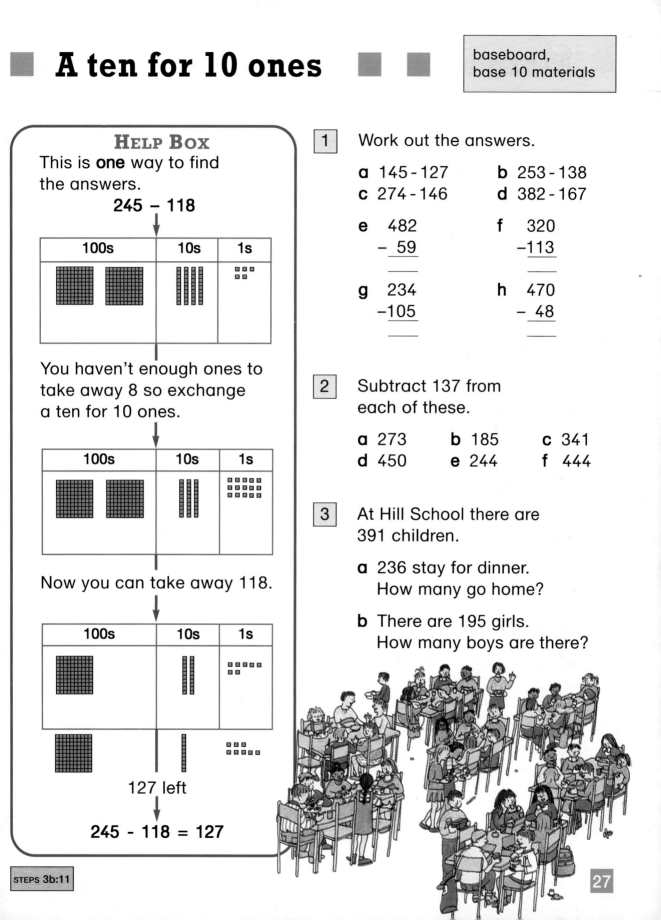

More exchanging

1. Decide the best way to find the answers.

   a 343 − 171
   b 253 − 182
   c 156 − 72

   d   409
         −236
         ‾‾‾‾

   e   327
         −273
         ‾‾‾‾

   f   156
         − 80
         ‾‾‾‾

2. Subtract 163 from each of these.

   a 234   **b** 258   **c** 306   **d** 415   **e** 327   **f** 409

3. Find the two subtractions that each have a mistake. Write them correctly.

   a   405
         − 72
         ‾‾‾‾
          333

   b   346
         − 64
         ‾‾‾‾
          382

   c   274
         −167
         ‾‾‾‾
          107

   d   425
         −372
         ‾‾‾‾
           53

   e   290
         − 47
         ‾‾‾‾
          243

   f   341
         −277
         ‾‾‾‾
          164

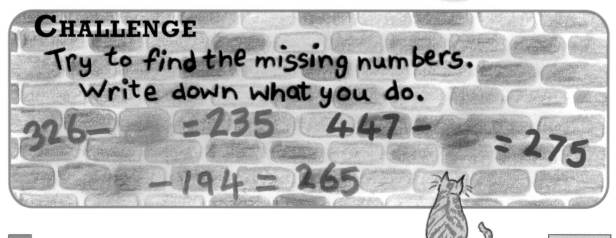

Oops! I've made one mistake.

So have I! One of my answers is silly.

CHALLENGE

Try to find the missing numbers. Write down what you do.

326 − ⬚ = 235   447 − ⬚ = 275

⬚ − 194 = 265

Checking subtraction

baseboard,
base 10 materials

A Bill's dad had 40 beakers in his cafe.

B He used 18 of them for teas and coffees. How many were left?

40 − 18 = 22

C Dad washed the dirty beakers and Bill put them back.

22 + 18 = 40

You can check subtractions like this:

40 − 18 = 22
22 + 18 = 40

---

1 Do these subtractions and then check by adding.

   a 268 − 137   **b** 356 − 143   **c** 480 − 34

   d 379 − 106   **e** 176 − 25   **f** 499 − 333

2 Make up four subtractions of your own. Then check by adding.

3 Write and illustrate a story like the one shown above.
Use these numbers: 25 15 10

Colourful fractions

1   For each shape **a** to **g**, write the fraction that is coloured.

a

b

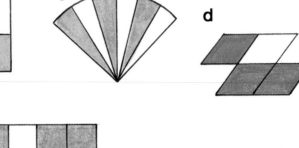
c

d

e

f
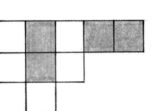

g

2   For each shape, **a** to **g**, write the fraction that is **not** coloured.

For shape **a**
Sam wrote   → $\frac{4}{5}$ is red.
$\frac{1}{5}$ is white.
$\frac{4}{5} + \frac{1}{5} = \frac{5}{5} = 1$

3   Write about the shapes **b** to **g** in the same way as Sam.

What is the same about all of these?
$\frac{4}{4}$ $\frac{5}{5}$ $\frac{6}{6}$ $\frac{7}{7}$ $\frac{8}{8}$ $\frac{10}{10}$

CHALLENGE

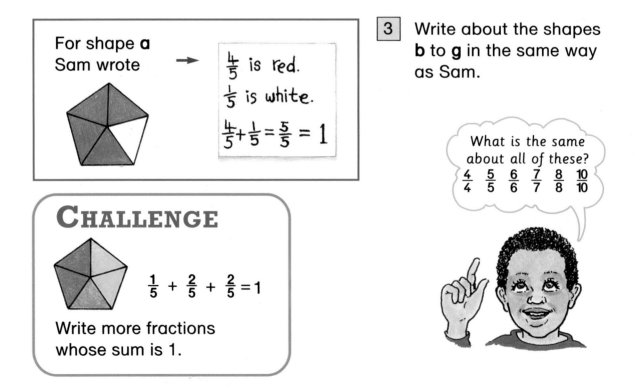

$\frac{1}{5} + \frac{2}{5} + \frac{2}{5} = 1$

Write more fractions whose sum is 1.

Equal divisions ■ ■ ■ ■ ■ ■

Paul drew a line 15 cm long. He divided it into 3 equal parts.

|← 5 cm | 5 cm | 5 cm →|

He wrote: $\frac{1}{3}$ of 15 cm = 5 cm   is the same as ←——→   15 cm ÷ 3 = 5 cm

1 Draw lines of these lengths. Divide them into 3 equal parts. Write about each one in the same way as Paul did.

a 6 cm   **b** 9 cm   **c** 12 cm

2 Draw lines of these lengths, Divide them into 4 equal parts. Write about each one in the same way.

a 8 cm   **b** 16 cm   **c** 20 cm

3 Choose 4 more lines to draw. Divide them into equal parts. Write about them in the same way.

4 Write a story about this picture.

Try to use all these words.

It's not fair!

★quarter ★half
★three-quarters
★whole ★share
★happy ★sad
★equal ★fair

Sliding about

1. Get some wax crayons (or chalks) 3 cm to 4 cm long.

2. Try to make shapes like these by sliding your crayons on their sides **without turning them**.

3. a

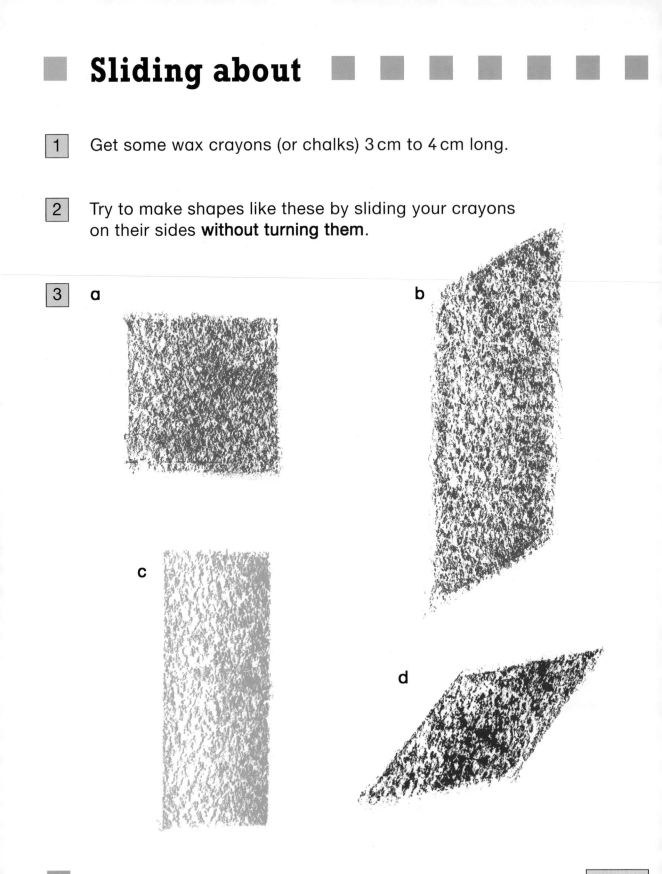

b

c

d

4 Now try these. They are harder!

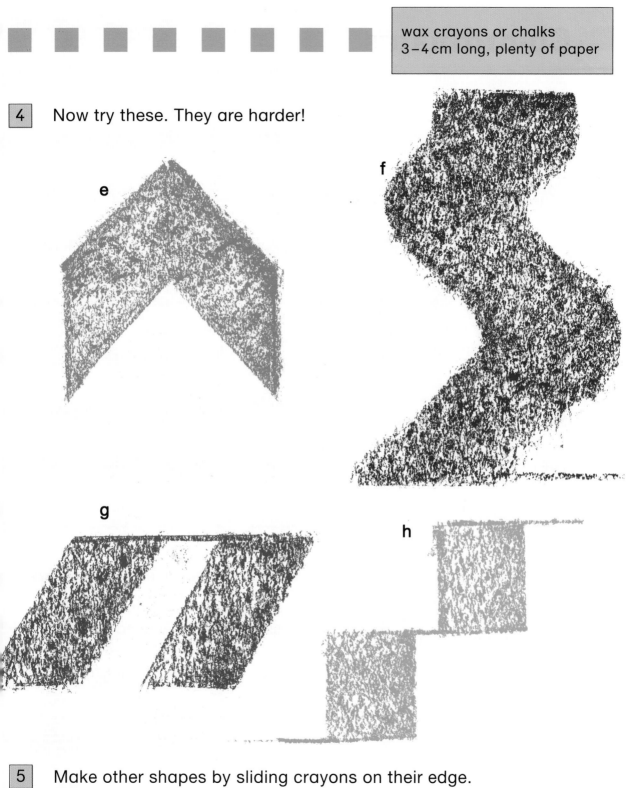

e

f

g

h

5 Make other shapes by sliding crayons on their edge.
Can your friends copy them?

Co-ordinates

Wildlife Park

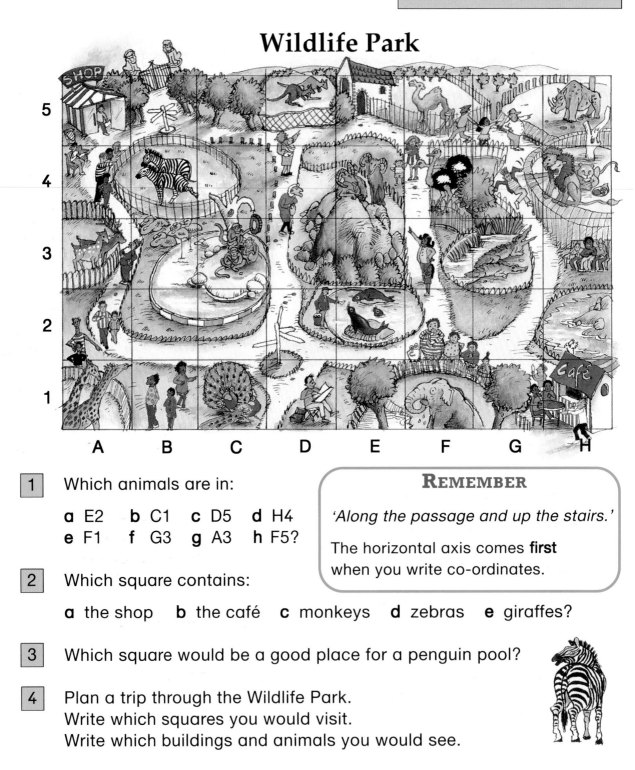

1 Which animals are in:

    a E2 **b** C1 **c** D5 **d** H4
    e F1 **f** G3 **g** A3 **h** F5?

> **REMEMBER**
>
> *'Along the passage and up the stairs.'*
>
> The horizontal axis comes **first** when you write co-ordinates.

2 Which square contains:

    a the shop **b** the café **c** monkeys **d** zebras **e** giraffes?

3 Which square would be a good place for a penguin pool?

4 Plan a trip through the Wildlife Park.
Write which squares you would visit.
Write which buildings and animals you would see.

Holiday Island

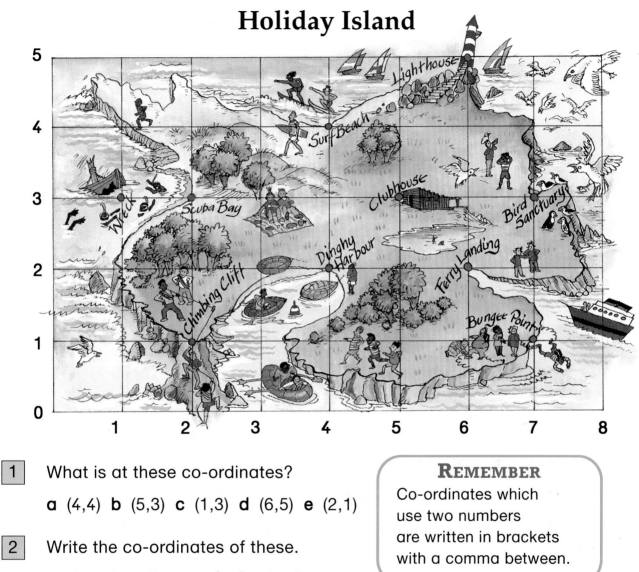

1   What is at these co-ordinates?

   a (4,4) **b** (5,3) **c** (1,3) **d** (6,5) **e** (2,1)

2   Write the co-ordinates of these.

   a Ferry Landing   **b** Scuba Bay
   c Bird Sanctuary   **d** Bungee Point   **e** Dinghy Harbour

3   Make up a map of your own on 2 cm squared paper.
   Write co-ordinates in figures along the axes.
   Write six questions about your map using co-ordinates.
   Can your friend answer your questions?

Pinboard areas

HELP BOX

These shapes enclose areas of:

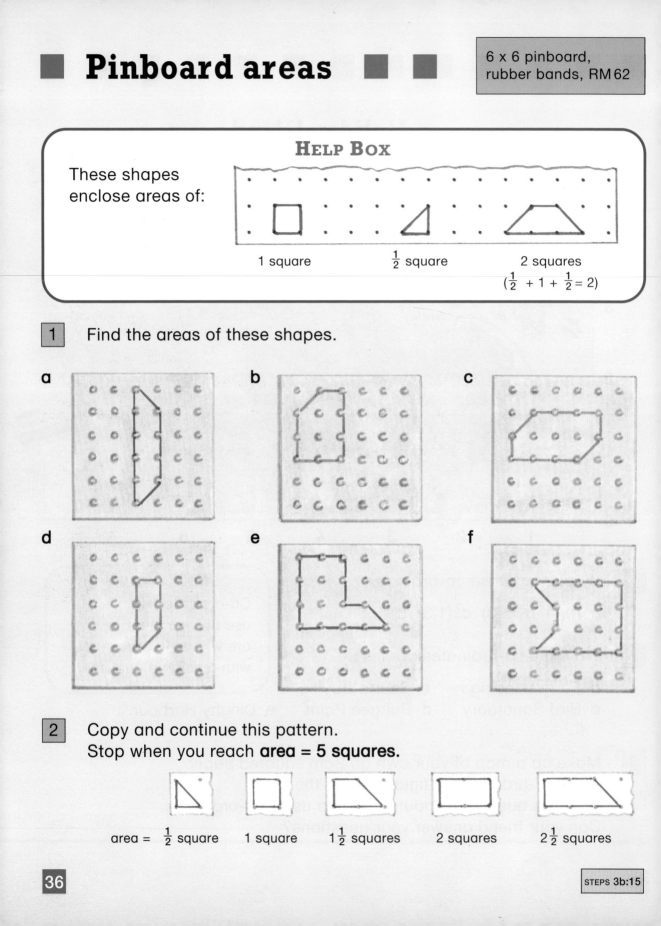

1 square $\frac{1}{2}$ square   2 squares

$(\frac{1}{2} + 1 + \frac{1}{2} = 2)$

1   Find the areas of these shapes.

a   b   c

d   e   f

2   Copy and continue this pattern.
Stop when you reach **area = 5 squares.**

area = $\frac{1}{2}$ square   1 square $1\frac{1}{2}$ squares   2 squares $2\frac{1}{2}$ squares

36

3 Make shapes of areas **a** to **i** on your pinboard.
Use RM 62 to draw and write about each shape you make. Like this:

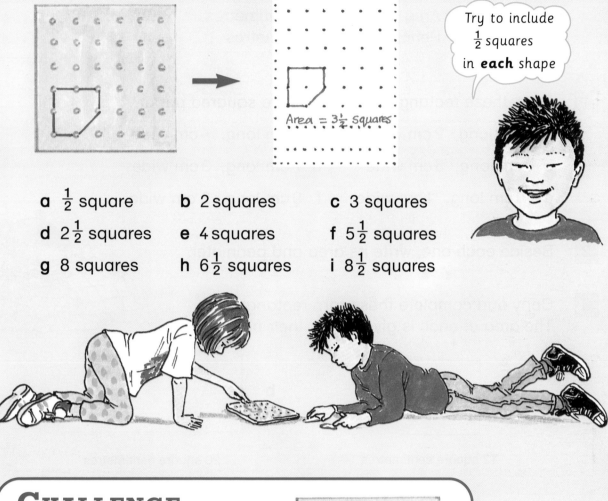

Area = 3½ squares

*Try to include ½ squares in **each** shape*

a ½ square

b 2 squares

c 3 squares

d 2½ squares

e 4 squares

f 5½ squares

g 8 squares

h 6½ squares

i 8½ squares

CHALLENGE

This shape has an area of 4½ squares.

Find and draw other shapes with the same area.

Area of rectangles

Do you agree?

This rectangle is
5 cm long and 3 cm wide.

Area = 15 square centimetres.
Perimeter = 16 centimetres

1 Draw these rectangles on centimetre squared paper.

   a 8 cm long, 2 cm wide   **b** 6 cm long, 4 cm wide

   c 6 cm long, 5 cm wide   **d** 7 cm long, 3 cm wide

   e 10 cm long, 1 cm wide   **f** 9 cm long, 2 cm wide

2 Beside each one, write its area and perimeter.

3 Copy and complete these torn rectangles.
The area of each is given. Find their perimeters.

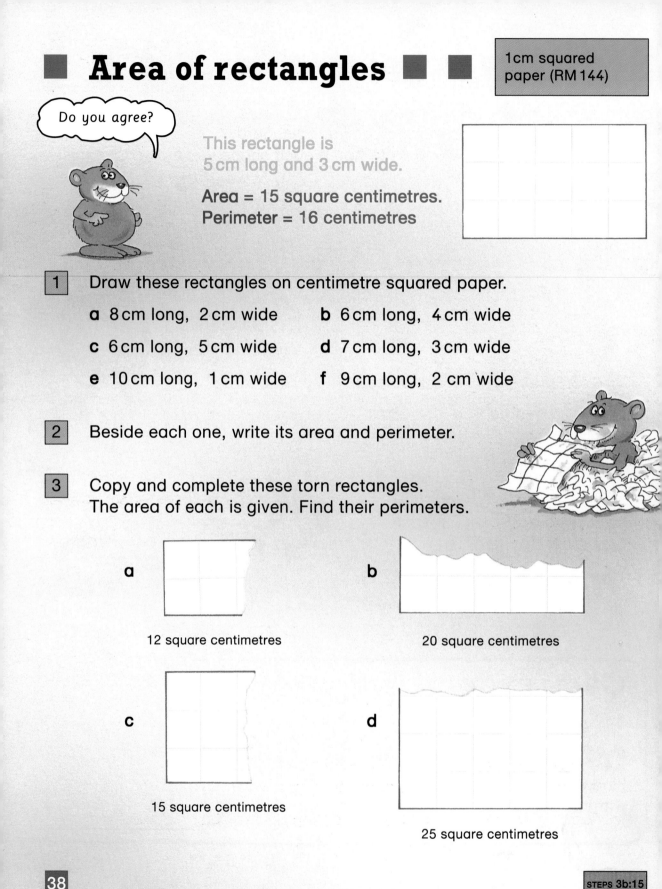

a

12 square centimetres

b

20 square centimetres

c

15 square centimetres

d

25 square centimetres

Balancing weights

balance scales, rice, plastic bag

These are standard weights up to 500g.

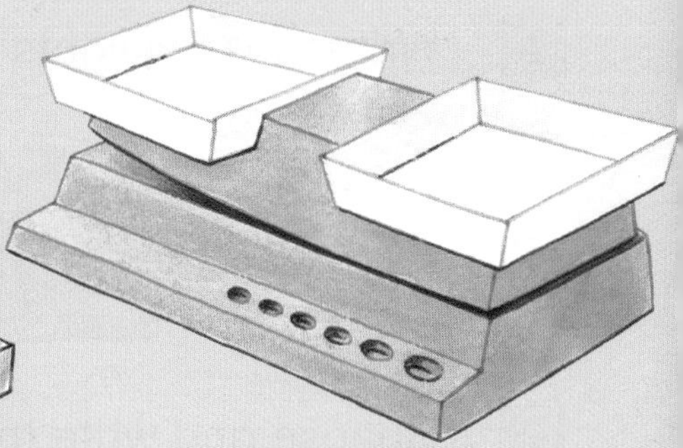

1g   5g   10g   20g   50g   100g   200g   500g

1 Write five ways to balance 50g using these standard weights.

2 Use scales and a plastic bag. Weigh out 70g of rice into a bag. Label the bag.

70g

3 Write five ways to balance 70g of rice using the weights shown above.

4 Copy and complete.

a Three standard weights which balance 500g are
_____ g and _____ g and _____ g.

b Four standard weights which balance 130g are
_____ g and _____ g and _____ g and _____ g.

CHALLENGE

Use **only** balance scales, a 20g weight and Plasticine.
Work out ways to make lumps of Plasticine which weigh:

a 80g   **b** 50g   **c** 10g   **d** 40g   **e** 25g   **f** 5g

Sensible weights

1 Write these weights in order, smallest first.

900g 150g 1kg100g 510g 15g

2 Choose and write the best estimate of the weight of each of these:

a
5g 50g 500g

b
15g 150g 1kg

c
1g 10g 20g

d
8g 80g 800g

e
1g 10g 100g

f
3g 30g 300g

g
20g 200g 2kg

h
7g 70g 700g

CHALLENGE

Can you think of **at least** three things which will weigh:

a about 10g   **b** about 50g   **c** about 100g?

Write or draw them in your book.

> Perhaps you could test some of them to see if you were right.

Buying games

■ ■ ■

coins, notes, money line, calculator

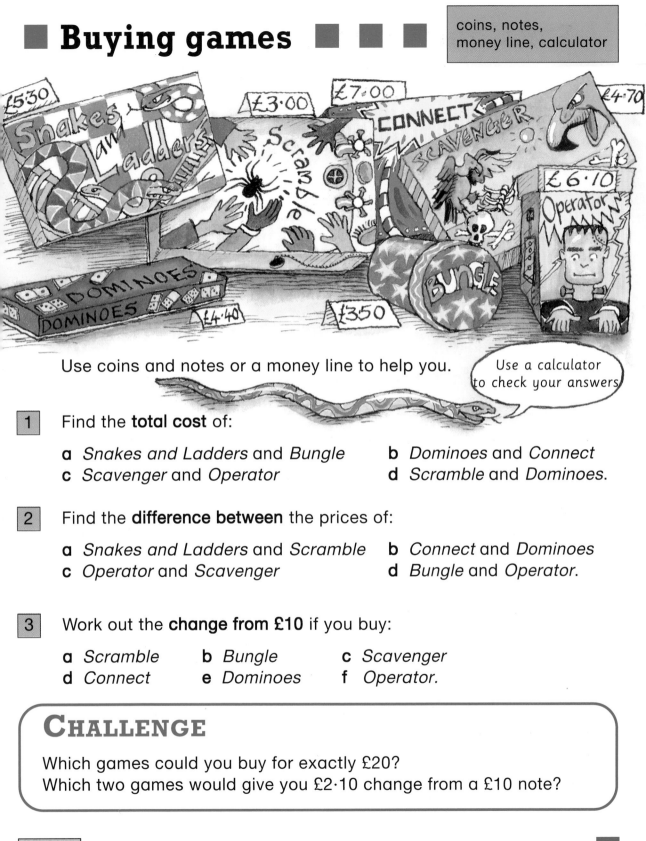

Use coins and notes or a money line to help you.

Use a calculator to check your answers

1 Find the **total cost** of:

    a *Snakes and Ladders* and *Bungle*   **b** *Dominoes* and *Connect*
    c *Scavenger* and *Operator*   **d** *Scramble* and *Dominoes*.

2 Find the **difference between** the prices of:

    a *Snakes and Ladders* and *Scramble*   **b** *Connect* and *Dominoes*
    c *Operator* and *Scavenger*   **d** *Bungle* and *Operator*.

3 Work out the **change from £10** if you buy:

    a *Scramble*   **b** *Bungle*   **c** *Scavenger*
    d *Connect*   **e** *Dominoes*   **f** *Operator*.

CHALLENGE

Which games could you buy for exactly £20?
Which two games would give you £2·10 change from a £10 note?

Stationery sales

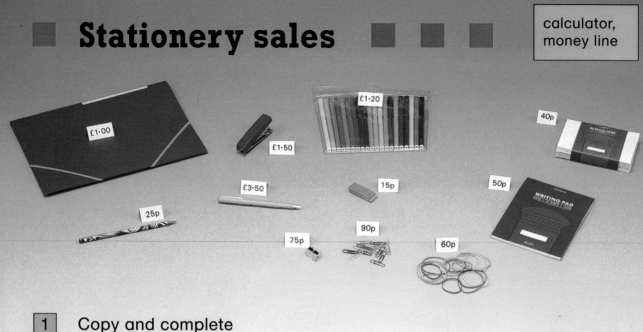

1 Copy and complete this ready reckoner.

Use a calculator or a money line.

	Erasers	Sharpener	Felt-tip pens
1	£0·15	£0·75	£1·20
2	£0·30	£1·50	£2·40
3	£0·45	£2·25	£3·60
4	·		
5	·		
6	·		
7	·		
8	·		
9	·		
10	·		

2 What is the cost of:

a 3 pencil sharpeners **b** 4 folders **c** 5 writing pads
d 4 packets of paper clips **e** 2 fountain pens **f** 3 staplers?

3 **a** How many pencils can I buy with £1·25?
b How many packets of envelopes can I buy with £1·60?
c How many pencil sharpeners can I buy with £3·00?

Multiplying money

1 Write how many coins or notes you need to make £10.
The first one is done for you.

a
2

b
—

c
—

d
—

e
—

f
—

2 Copy and complete this pattern.

£1   x 5 =
£1·50 x 5 =
£2   x 5 =
£2·50 x 5 =
£3   x 5 =
£3·50 x 5 =
£4   x 5 =
£4·50 x 5 =
£5   x 5 =

3 Ravi, Spiro and Maria are given this money to share equally.
Work out in your own way how much each would get.

50P —
20P —
10P —
5P —
-P — 3

Cube volumes

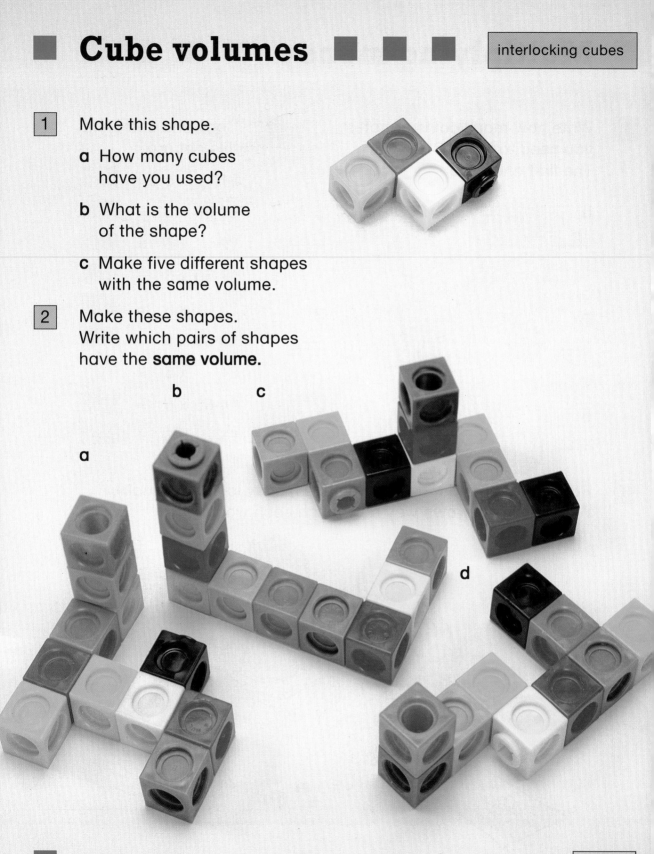

1 Make this shape.

   a How many cubes
      have you used?

   b What is the volume
      of the shape?

   c Make five different shapes
      with the same volume.

2 Make these shapes.
   Write which pairs of shapes
   have the **same volume.**

b

c

a

d

Circle patterns

gummed paper circles,
black pen

1 Cut some circles into
   halves and quarters.

2 Make them into patterns,
   then decorate with black pens.
   Here are some examples — but try not to copy!

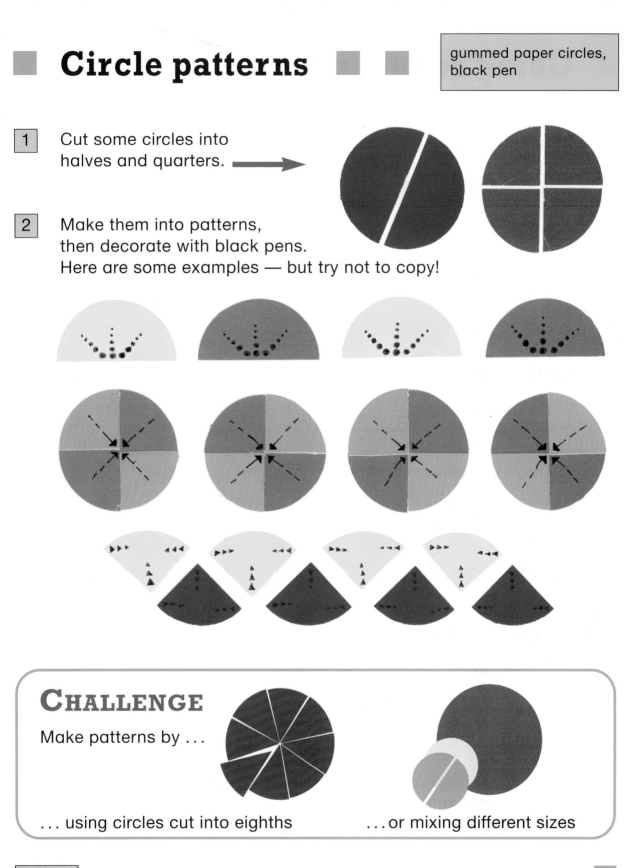

CHALLENGE

Make patterns by ...

... using circles cut into eighths   ...or mixing different sizes

Going round in circles

compasses, large sheet of paper

1 Make a pattern with arcs and circles.

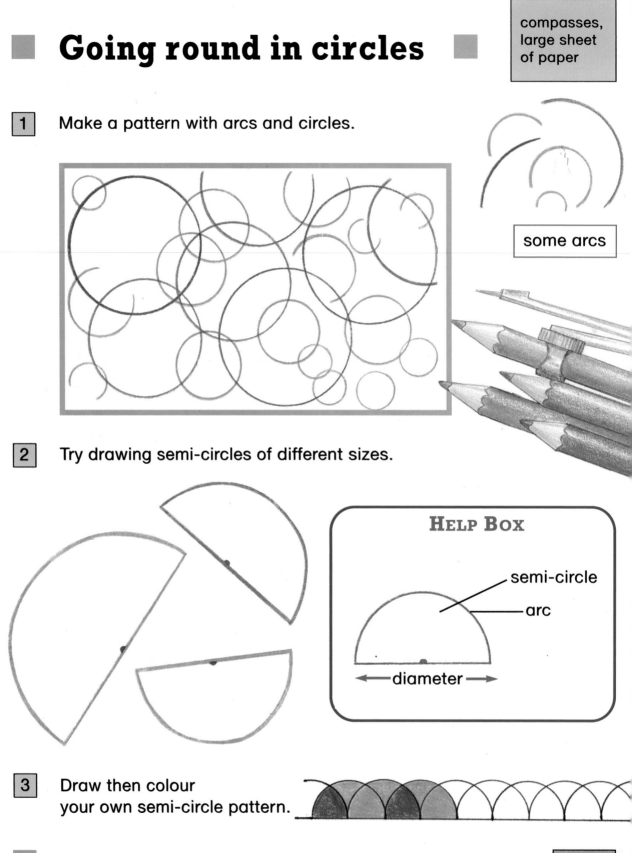

some arcs

2 Try drawing semi-circles of different sizes.

HELP BOX

semi-circle

arc

diameter

3 Draw then colour your own semi-circle pattern.

Symmetrical patterns

1cm squared paper
(RM 144), mirror

1 Place your mirror on the dotted line.
Is this pattern symmetrical? ➡️

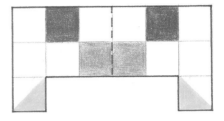

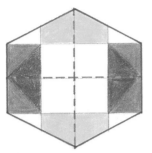

2 In this pattern there are
two lines of symmetry.
Check with your mirror. ⬅️

3 Copy each pattern onto squared paper. Colour the empty parts
to make the patterns symmetrical. You can use a mirror to help.

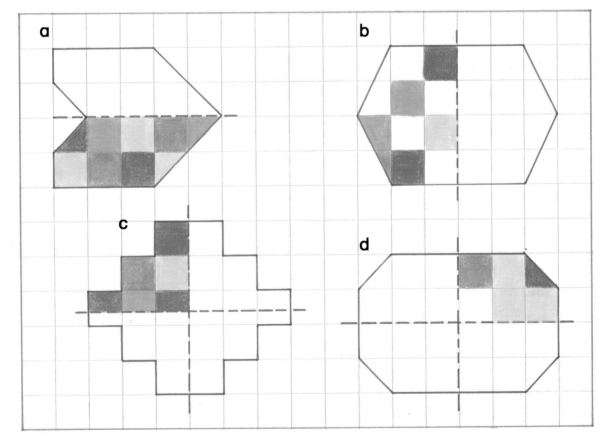

a

b

c

d

Symmetry puzzle

1

Use a mirror
on this shape
to find shapes
a to **h**.

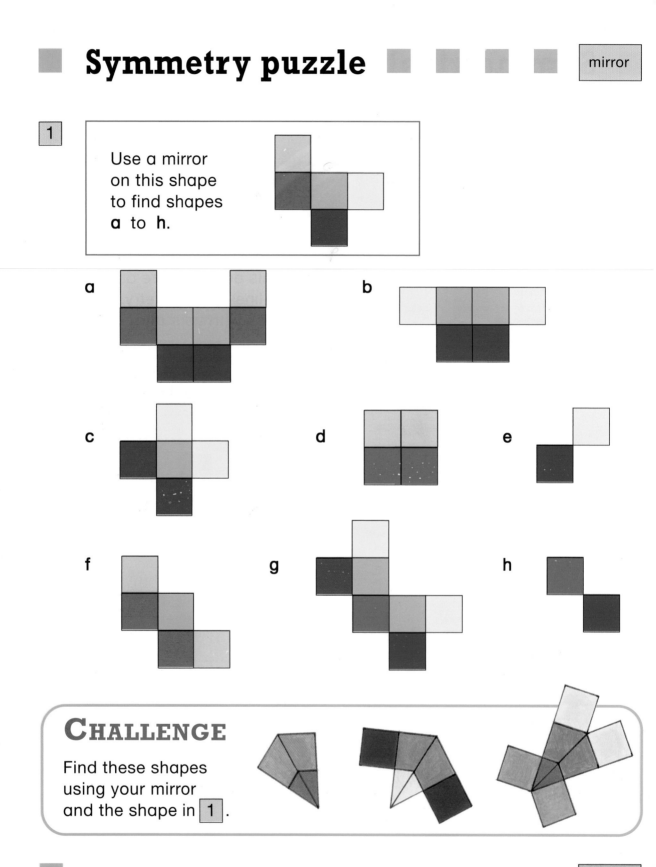

a

b

c

d

e

f

g

h

CHALLENGE

Find these shapes
using your mirror
and the shape in **1**.

48

STEPS 3b:20

Paper folding

scissors, coloured paper (about 10 cm by 10 cm), glue

1 Start with a small sheet of paper folded in half.

Make **two cuts only** around the fold line to create a new symmetrical shape.

2 Try to make shapes like these in the same way. Glue them into your book.

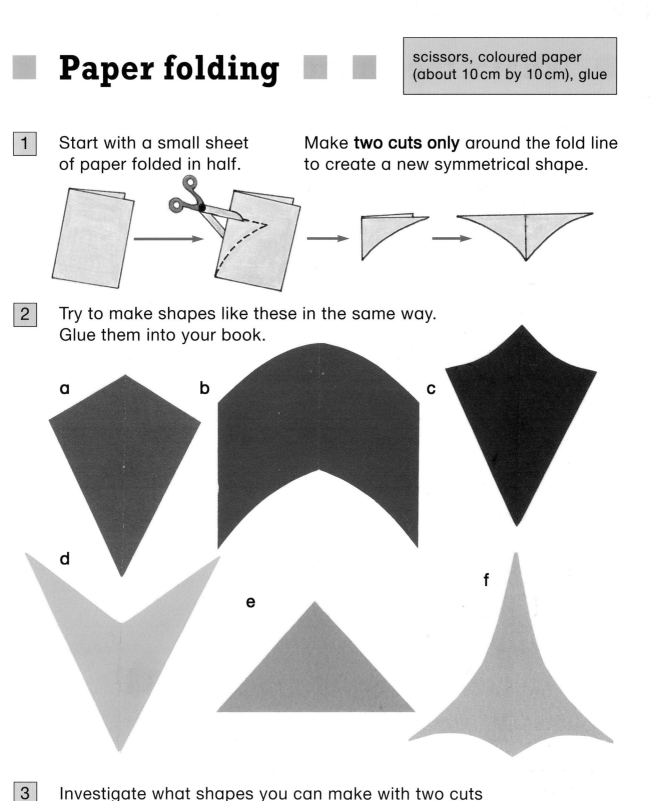

a

b

c

d

e

f

3 Investigate what shapes you can make with two cuts if you fold the paper in quarters.

What's the chance? ■ ■ ■ ■ ■

Jimmy, Ela, Morag and Gary
are playing a game.
They take turns to spin
a colour spinner.
If they spin the colour of their T-shirts,
they win a point.
The first to win 4 points
wins the game.

Jimmy

Gary

Ela

Morag

1 For this spinner, write:

   a who has the best chance of winning?
   b who has the poorest chance of winning?
   c which players have
      an equal chance of winning?

Now do the same for these spinners.

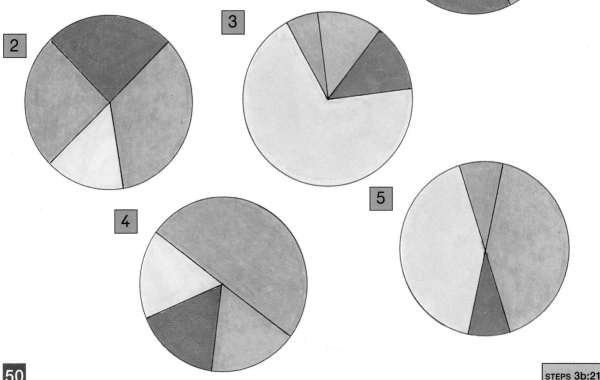

2

3

4

5

coloured stickers, blank dice

6 Design two more spinners, **a** and **b**.

Spinner **a**: Each player has an **equal** chance of winning.

Spinner **b**: Jimmy and Ela have a **good** chance of winning but Morag and Gary have a **poor** chance.

7 Use stickers in two colours and a blank dice.

1 Make a dice using both colours, one sticker on each face.

2 Predict how many times each colour will occur in 60 rolls.

3 Write down your prediction.

4 Make 60 rolls and, each time, keep a note of the colour. (Choose your own way to do this).

5 Afterwards, write the total number of rolls for each colour. Was your prediction nearly right?

What if we used 3 colours of stickers instead?

Table graphs

Lucy drew this graph showing the '2 x' and 'x 2' tables.

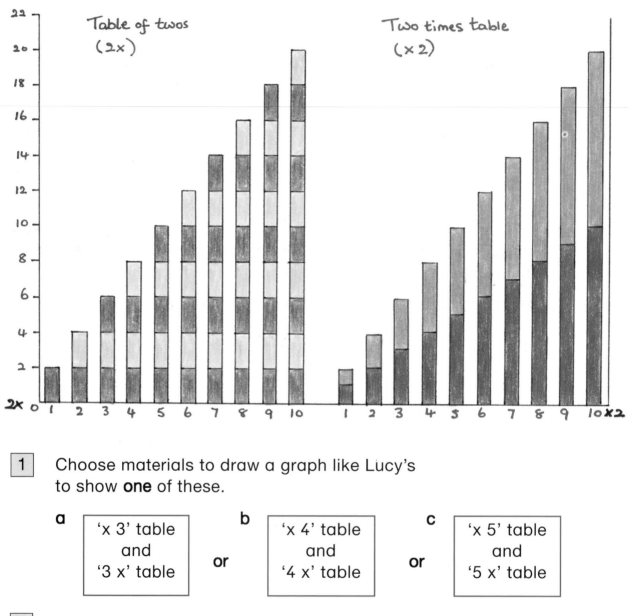

Table of twos
(2x)

Two times table
(x 2)

1   Choose materials to draw a graph like Lucy's
to show **one** of these.

a
'x 3' table
and
'3 x' table

or

b
'x 4' table
and
'4 x' table

or

c
'x 5' table
and
'5 x' table

2   Now work out which answers are in both
the 'x 2' table and the table you drew.
Show how you do this.

Multiplication

calculator,
completed copy of RM 89

1 Copy and complete.

   a   3 x 5 = 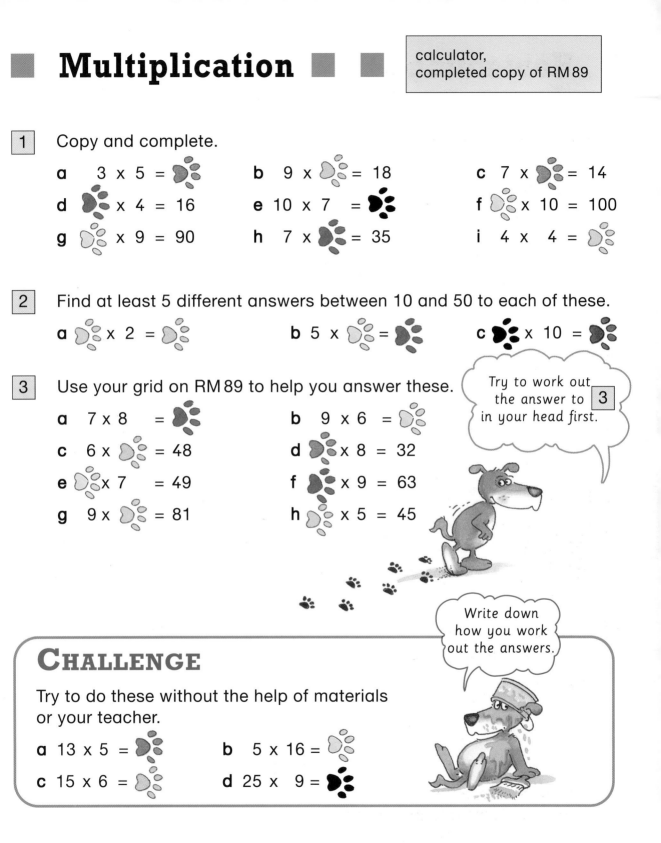   **b** 9 x   = 18   **c** 7 x   = 14

   d   x 4 = 16   **e** 10 x 7 =   **f**   x 10 = 100

   g   x 9 = 90   **h** 7 x   = 35   **i** 4 x 4 =

2 Find at least 5 different answers between 10 and 50 to each of these.

   a   x 2 =   **b** 5 x   =   **c**   x 10 =

3 Use your grid on RM 89 to help you answer these.

> Try to work out the answer to **3** in your head first.

   a 7 x 8   =   **b** 9 x 6 =

   c 6 x   = 48   **d**   x 8 = 32

   e   x 7   = 49   **f**   x 9 = 63

   g 9 x   = 81   **h**   x 5 = 45

> Write down how you work out the answers.

CHALLENGE

Try to do these without the help of materials
or your teacher.

   a 13 x 5 =   **b** 5 x 16 =

   c 15 x 6 =   **d** 25 x 9 =

How much? How many?

1 Find the cost of these:

   a 7 stamps at 6p each   **b** 9 stamps at 5p each
   c 8 stamps at 4p each   **d** 7 stamps at 3p each
   e 5 stamps at 3p **and** 8 stamps at 6p each
   f 8 stamps at 10p **and** 6 stamps at 2p each.

2 Try to find the cost of these without a calculator.
Write down what you do.

   a 5 pencils at 14p each   **b** 6 mini-bars at 11p each
   c 7 apples at 12p each   **d** 5 comics at 18p each
   e 4 dice at 16p each   **f** 12 marbles at 8p each

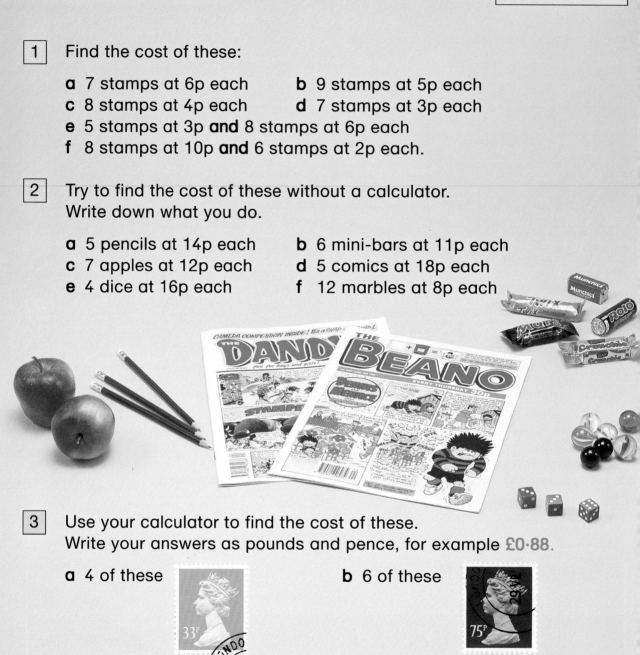

3 Use your calculator to find the cost of these.
Write your answers as pounds and pence, for example £0·88.

   a 4 of these    **b** 6 of these

   c 8 of these   **d** 20 of these

Split and multiply

Here are 10 rows of 5 stickers.

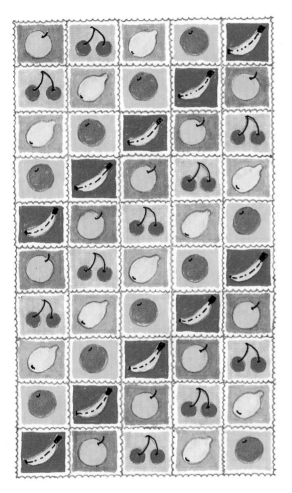

5 x 10 = 50

1 Use your straw to split the block of stickers into 6 rows and 4 rows.

You can write about it like this.

$(5 \times 6) + (5 \times 4)$
$= 30 + 20$
$= 50$

2 Now split the stickers in each of these ways. Write about each one.

a 5 rows and 5 rows
b 3 rows and 7 rows
c 8 rows and 2 rows
d 1 row and 9 rows

3 Draw six more boxes like this to show different ways of splitting groups of two.

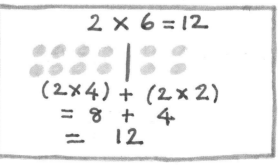

$2 \times 6 = 12$

$(2 \times 4) + (2 \times 2)$
$= 8 + 4$
$= 12$

Writing decimals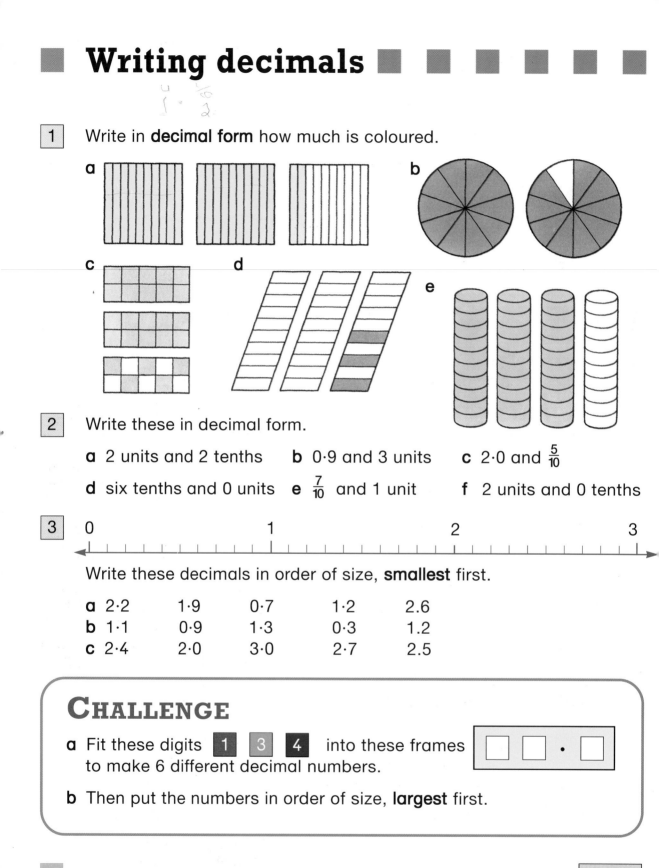

1 Write in **decimal form** how much is coloured.

a

b

c

d

e

2 Write these in decimal form.

a 2 units and 2 tenths   **b** 0·9 and 3 units   **c** 2·0 and $\frac{5}{10}$

d six tenths and 0 units   **e** $\frac{7}{10}$ and 1 unit   **f** 2 units and 0 tenths

3

```
0                    1                    2                    3
```

Write these decimals in order of size, **smallest** first.

a 2·2   1·9   0·7   1·2   2·6
b 1·1   0·9   1·3   0·3   1.2
c 2·4   2·0   3·0   2·7   2.5

CHALLENGE

a Fit these digits 1 3 4 into these frames ☐☐·☐
to make 6 different decimal numbers.

b Then put the numbers in order of size, **largest** first.

Adding decimals

base 10 materials, decimal abacus, RM 95, calculator

Choose materials to help you with 1 and 2 .

1   Add these decimals.

    a $0.3 + 1.3$ **b** $2.6 + 0.7$ **c** $4.8 + 1.7$
    d $2.8 + 4.2$ **e** $6.9 + 1.7$ **f** $3.3 + 6.6$
    g $2.5 + 4.5$ **h** $5.7 + 0.9$ **i** $3.2 + 4.9$

2   Find at least 5 pairs of numbers which total 2·4.

3   Experiment on your calculator to find out
    what is missing on the blank keys. Write your answers.

    a   1 · 4 + ☐ ☐ ☐ =   `3.6`

    b   ☐ ☐ ☐ + 2 · 5 =   `9.8`

    c   1 · 8 + ☐ ☐ ☐ =   `5.4`

    d   ☐ ☐ ☐ + 6 · 4 =   `10.`

4   Investigate. Use these keys 2 3 4 5
    as often as you like to go here:

    ☐ · ☐ + ☐ · ☐ =

Here is one way you might find.

    Make the calculator display as
    many different answers as you can.
    Record your additions.

2·3 + 4·5 = 6·8

Subtracting decimals

base 10 materials,
decimal abacus,
RM 95, calculator

Choose materials
to help you.

We've
found a pair!

1 Subtract these decimals without using a calculator.

a 0·8 – 0·3   b 1·6 – 0·5   c 2·7 – 1·2
d 6·6 – 5·7   e 5·0 – 1·8   f 8·0 – 4·7

2 Find at least 5 pairs of numbers
with a difference of 0·6.

2·7   2·1

3 Experiment on your calculator to find out
what is missing on the blank keys. Write your answers.

a 5 · 6 ▢ ▢ ▢ ▢ =   3.6

b 8 · 4 ▢ ▢ ▢ ▢ =   2.7

c ▢ ▢ ▢ ▢ 2 · 2 =   8.5

4 Now try these.

a Jack ran a race in 8·4 seconds, Mena was 1·5 seconds faster.
What was Mena's time?

b Ginger's tail is 6.3 cm long, Whiskey's tail is 4.2 cm long.
How much longer is Ginger's tail than Whiskey's?

CHALLENGE

Start
write a decimal → add 2·1 → subtract 0·7 → add 1·4 → subtract 2·8 →

Follow these rules.
Write about what happens.

STEPS 3b:23

Nets for cubes

6 Polydron or Clixi squares, squared paper, triangular dotty paper (RM 148)

Work with a partner if you can.

1 Join six squares to form a 'hexomino'. Can you fold the hexomino to make a **closed** cube?

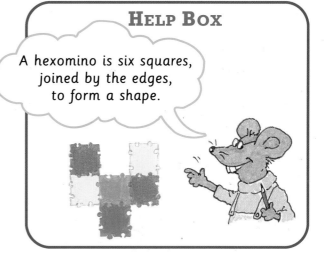

HELP BOX

A hexomino is six squares, joined by the edges, to form a shape.

2 Try different hexominoes.

3 Record your results on squared paper, like this:

Will this fold to make a cube?

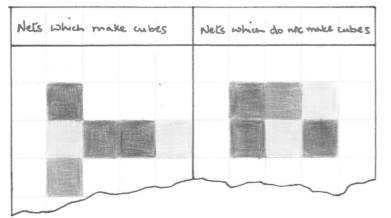

Nets which make cubes	Nets which do not make cubes

CHALLENGE

Get some triangular dotty paper. Try drawing and colouring cubes of different sizes.

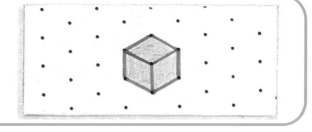

Model creatures

Polydron or Clixi
squares and triangles,
Blu-Tack, round stickers

Try to work with others in a group.

1 Make a shared supply of:

cubes   tetrahedra   square-based pyramids

2 Put or stick these together in different ways and add eyes (stickers)
to make them into strange creatures.
Here are some:

3 Give each creature a letter.

4 In your book, design a table
to show how many of each shape
were used to make each creature.

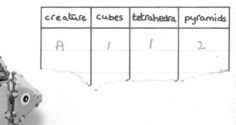

creature	cubes	tetrahedra	pyramids
A	1	1	2

5 Compare your table with others in your group.

Recognising shapes

1 Find as many examples of these shapes as you can.

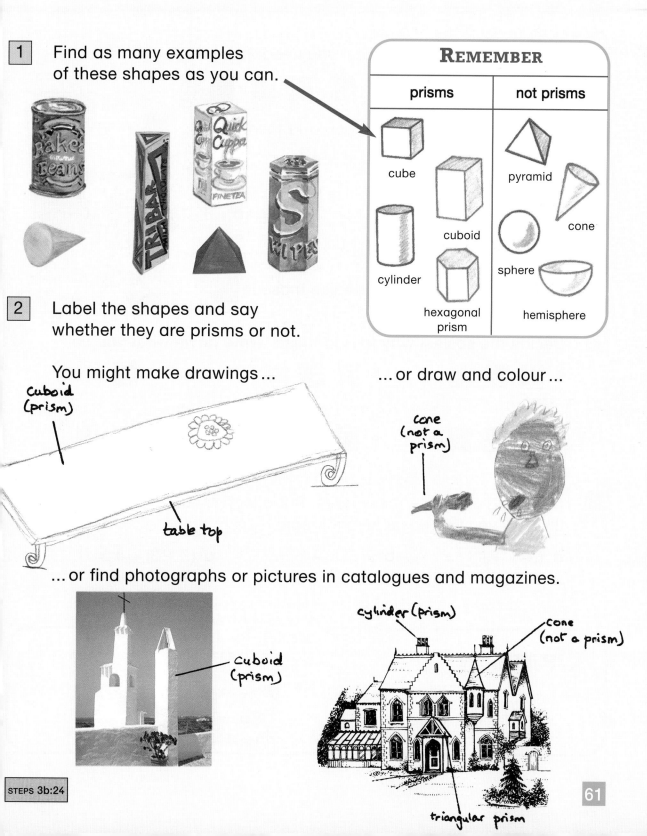

REMEMBER	
prisms	**not prisms**
cube	pyramid
cuboid	cone
cylinder	sphere
hexagonal prism	hemisphere

2 Label the shapes and say whether they are prisms or not.

You might make drawings...

cuboid (prism)

table top

... or draw and colour...

cone (not a prism)

... or find photographs or pictures in catalogues and magazines.

cuboid (prism)

cylinder (prism)

cone (not a prism)

triangular prism

Order of adding

Use cards like these to help you if you need them.

| 0 | 1 | 2 | 3 | 4 | 5 | 6 | 7 | 8 | 9 |

1 Gather up the tens to help you add these.

> This is one way of **gathering 10**.

a 3 + 7 + 4   **b** 4 + 6 + 8

c 8 + 8 + 2   **d** 9 + 1 + 9

e 5 + 7 + 3   **f** 10 + 0 + 7

> 3 + 7 + 5
> = (3 + 7) + 5
> = 10 + 5
> = 15

2 Make up six more examples like those in **1**.

3 Decide the easiest way to add these. Write down what you do.

a 3 8 7   **b** 4 8 6   **c** 9 8 1

d 6 7 4   **e** 5 9 5   **f** 7 5 3

4 Copy and complete these pairs. Put a loop round the way you find easier in each pair.

a (9 + 1) + 7 =   **b** (8 + 5) + 5 =   **c** (7 + 3) + 8 =
   9 + (1 + 7) =   8 + (5 + 5) =   7 + (3 + 8) =

CHALLENGE

> Make at least six more sums like this. The answer must be 20 each time

(4 + 6) + (7 + 3) = 20

■ > and < ■ ■ ■ ■ ■ ■

1 Copy and complete these.

a 8 + 5 =   b 9 + 4 =
c 7 + 6 =   d 7 + 9 =
e 11 + 7 =   f 14 + 5 =
g 17 + 3 =   h 13 + 6 =

Use the answers to help you
with the rest of the page.

REMEMBER

2 Write <, > or = instead of 🐾 to make each number sentence true.

a 8 + 5 🐾 7 + 9   b 11 + 7 🐾 8 + 5   c 7 + 6 🐾 9 + 4
d 13 + 6 🐾 14 + 5   e 17 + 3 🐾 11 + 7   f 11 + 7 🐾 7 + 6
g 9 + 4 🐾 13 + 6   h 14 + 5 🐾 17 + 3   i 8 + 5 🐾 9 + 4

3 Do these in the same way as **2**.

a 80 + 50 🐾 70 + 90   b 90 + 40 🐾 70 + 60
c 90 + 40 🐾 80 + 50   d 110 + 70 🐾 70 + 90
e 80 + 50 🐾 170 + 30   f 110 + 70 🐾 140 + 50

4 Copy this number snake and make it longer.
Use < and > or = and totals to 20.

3 + 4 > 0 + 2 < 8 + 4

Turning patterns

Polydron or
Clixi tiles,
squared paper

1 Copy and complete these patterns on squared paper.

Turn $\frac{1}{4}$ turn clockwise

a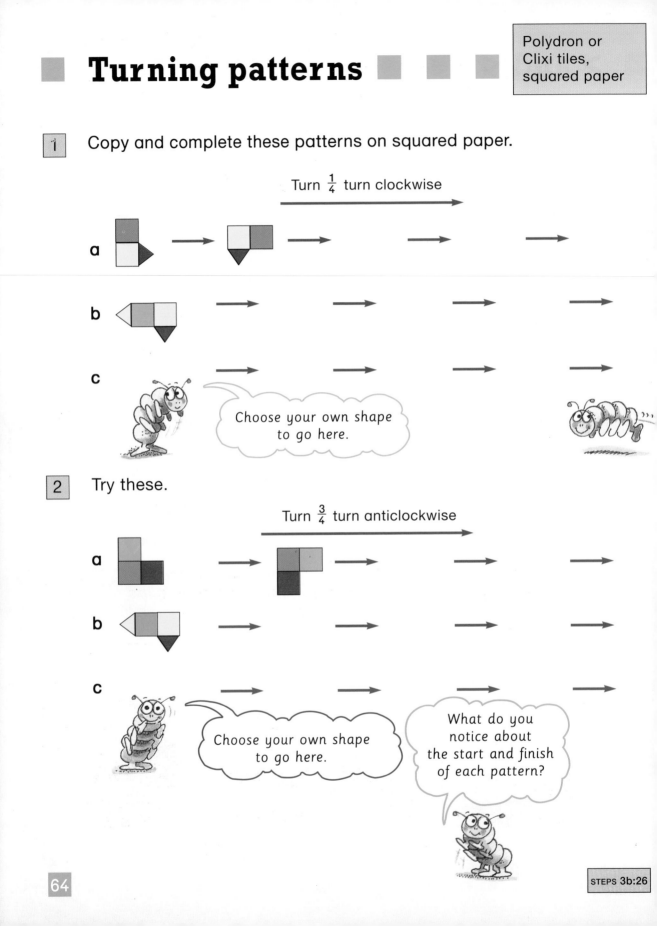

b

c Choose your own shape to go here.

2 Try these.

Turn $\frac{3}{4}$ turn anticlockwise

a

b

c Choose your own shape to go here.

What do you notice about the start and finish of each pattern?

Rotating shapes ■ ■ ■ ■

small white cards, glue

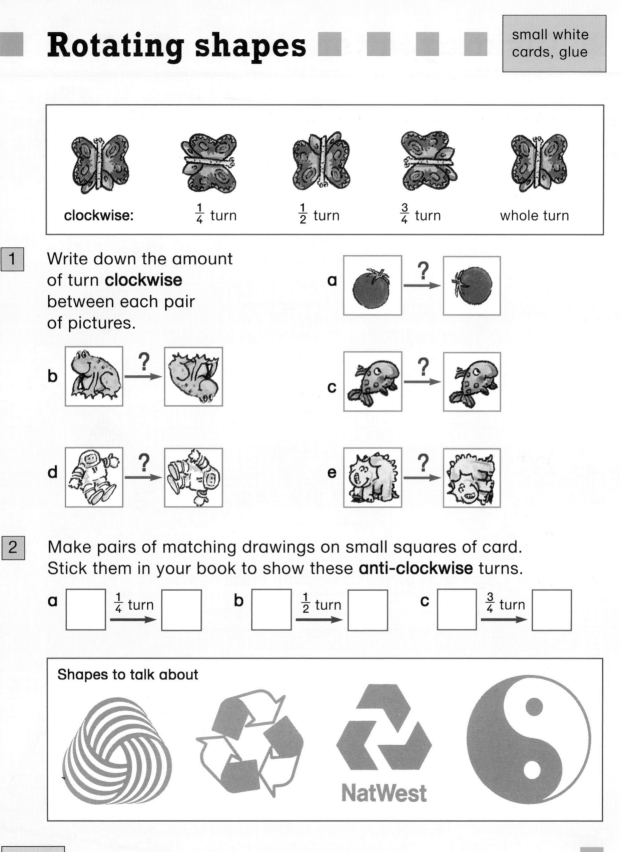

clockwise: $\frac{1}{4}$ turn $\frac{1}{2}$ turn $\frac{3}{4}$ turn   whole turn

1 Write down the amount of turn **clockwise** between each pair of pictures.

a

b

c

d

e

2 Make pairs of matching drawings on small squares of card. Stick them in your book to show these **anti-clockwise** turns.

a ☐ $\frac{1}{4}$ turn → ☐   b ☐ $\frac{1}{2}$ turn → ☐   c ☐ $\frac{3}{4}$ turn → ☐

Shapes to talk about

NatWest

Dividing in your head

■ ■ ■ ■

1　Polly made a
x and ÷ diamond.
Complete these diamonds
in the same way in your book.

$2 \times 10 = 20$

$20 \div 10 = 2$ $10 \times 2 = 20$

$20 \div 2 = 10$

a
$7 \times 5 = 35$

b
$8 \times 2 = 16$

c
$10 \times 4 = 40$

d
$45 \div 5 = 9$

e
$18 \div 9 = 2$

f
$70 \div 10 = 7$

2　Make 3 diamonds of your own using these numbers.

| 5 | 7 | 9 | 10 | 35 | 45 | 70 |

3　Try to work out the answers to these in your head.

a Share 40 cards between 4 players. How many cards each?

b Put 35 apples into bags, 5 in a bag. How many bags?

c Divide 18 sweets between 2 friends. How many each?

4　Write a story to show what this means: $40 \div 5 = 8$

$40 \div 5 = 8$

Sharing

1 Choose how to find the answers by sharing.

a 24 ÷ 2 =   **b** 44 ÷ 2 =
c 48 ÷ 2 =   **d** 62 ÷ 2 =
e 68 ÷ 2 =   **f** 86 ÷ 2 =

2 Now try these.

a 36 ÷ 3 =   **b** 55 ÷ 5 =
c 48 ÷ 4 =   **d** 69 ÷ 3 =
e 84 ÷ 4 =   **f** 93 ÷ 3 =

HELP BOX

This is one way of sharing.

28 ÷ 2

20 + 8

10 + 4   10 + 4

28 ÷ 2 = 14

3 Write the missing numbers.

a 28 fish shared between 2 penguins makes ____ each.

b 48 biscuits shared between 4 dogs makes ____ each.

c One third of 39 ants is ____ ants.

4 Make up more animal problems like those in **3** for friends to try.

Sharing and exchanging

1 Choose how to find these answers by sharing.

a $32 \div 2 =$

b $54 \div 2 =$

c $38 \div 2 =$

d $42 \div 3 =$

e $48 \div 3 =$

f $54 \div 3 =$

g $65 \div 5 =$

h $92 \div 4 =$

2 Write the missing numbers.

a One half of 34 bees makes _____ bees.

b 45 apples shared between 3 horses makes _____ apples each.

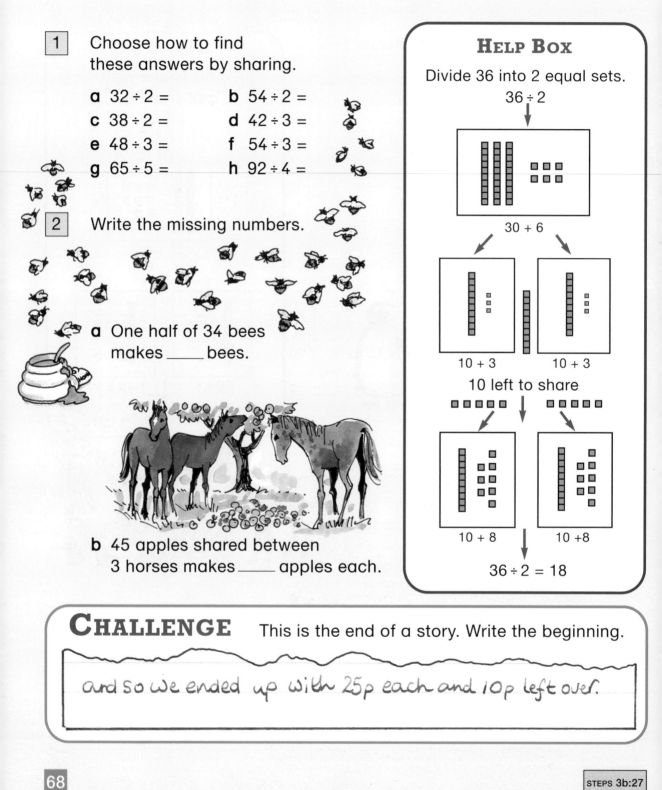

HELP BOX

Divide 36 into 2 equal sets.

$36 \div 2$

$30 + 6$

$10 + 3$ $10 + 3$

10 left to share

$10 + 8$ $10 + 8$

$36 \div 2 = 18$

CHALLENGE This is the end of a story. Write the beginning.

and so we ended up with 25p each and 10p left over.

Mental subtractions

1 Copy and complete these.

a 14 – 9   b 16 – 7
c 15 – 3   d 18 – 11
e 19 – 8   f 17 – 4
g 12 – 5   h 20 – 12

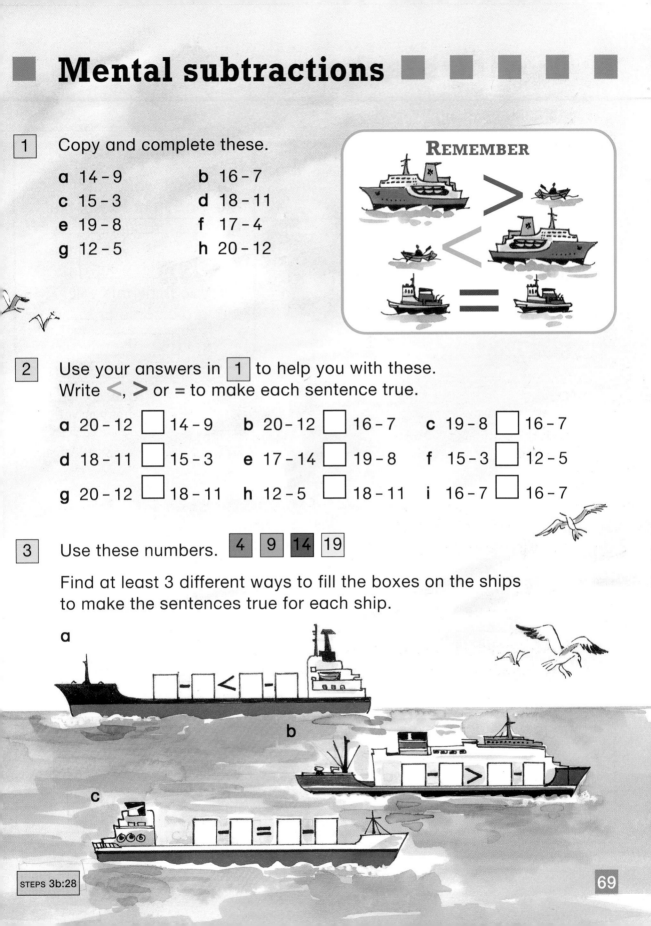

REMEMBER

2 Use your answers in ▢1 to help you with these.
Write <, > or = to make each sentence true.

a 20 – 12 ▢ 14 – 9   b 20 – 12 ▢ 16 – 7   c 19 – 8 ▢ 16 – 7

d 18 – 11 ▢ 15 – 3   e 17 – 14 ▢ 19 – 8   f 15 – 3 ▢ 12 – 5

g 20 – 12 ▢ 18 – 11   h 12 – 5 ▢ 18 – 11   i 16 – 7 ▢ 16 – 7

3 Use these numbers.   4   9   14   19

Find at least 3 different ways to fill the boxes on the ships
to make the sentences true for each ship.

a   ▢ – ▢ < ▢ – ▢

b   ▢ – ▢ > ▢ – ▢

c   ▢ – ▢ = ▢ – ▢

Moving brackets

1 **a** $(12 - 5) - 3 =$
   b $12 - (5 - 3) =$

Work out the answers to these and see what happens.

2 **a** $14 - (7 - 2) =$
   b $(14 - 7) - 2 =$

3 **a** $(15 - 8) - 1 =$
   b $15 - (8 - 1) =$

4 **a** $(20 - 10) - 10 =$
   b $20 - (10 - 10) =$

REMEMBER

You **must** work out the part in brackets **first**.

$$10 - (6 - 4)$$
$$= 10 - 2$$
$$= 8$$

Do you think this will have the same answer?

$$(10 - 6) - 4$$

What do you think will happen with these?

5 **a** $(12 - 5) + 3 =$
   b $12 - (5 + 3) =$

6 **a** $110 - (60 + 40) =$
   b $(110 - 60) + 40 =$

7 **a** $10 + (5 - 4) =$
   b $(10 + 5) - 4 =$

8 **a** $(120 - 40) + 30 =$
   b $120 - (40 + 30) =$

9 **a** $20 - (7 + 5) =$
   b $(20 - 7) + 5 =$

CHALLENGE

Use numbers up to 20 to go in the empty boxes.

Find as many ways as you can to make the answer of 9 correct.

$$17 - (\boxed{} - \boxed{}) = 9$$

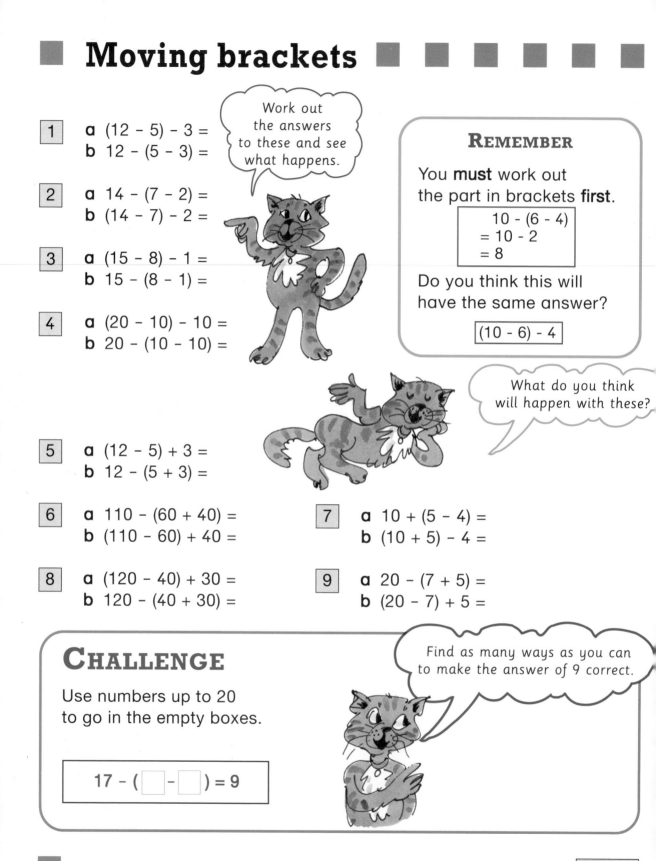

Number displays ■ ■ ■ ■

Use only the arrowed keys on your calculator.

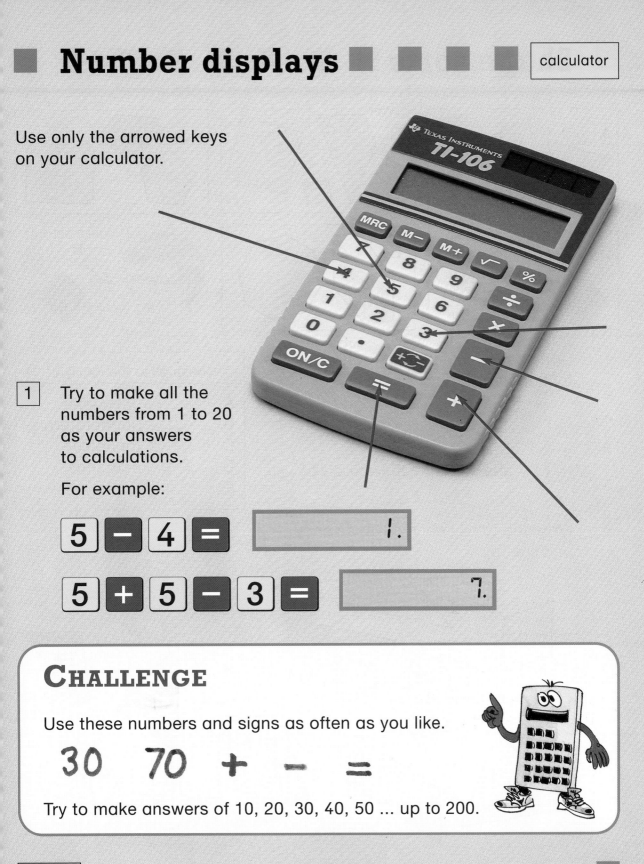

1 Try to make all the numbers from 1 to 20 as your answers to calculations.

For example:

| 5 | − | 4 | = | | |. |

| 5 | + | 5 | − | 3 | = | | 7. |

CHALLENGE

Use these numbers and signs as often as you like.

$$30 \quad 70 \quad + \quad - \quad =$$

Try to make answers of 10, 20, 30, 40, 50 ... up to 200.

Shape sorts

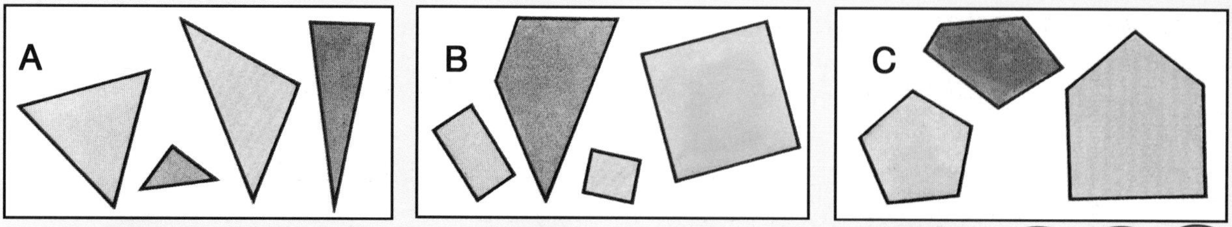

A

B

C

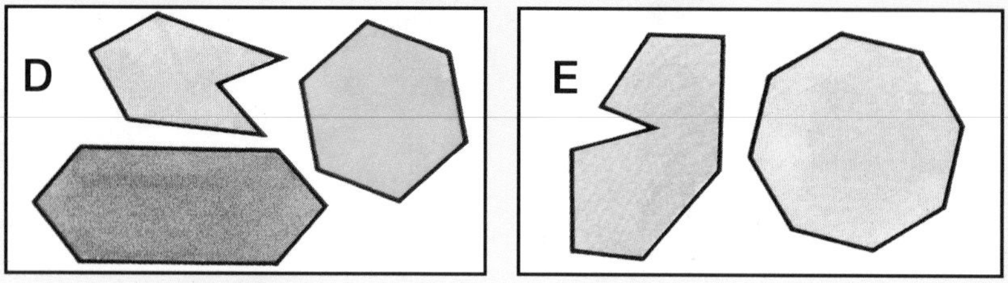

D

E

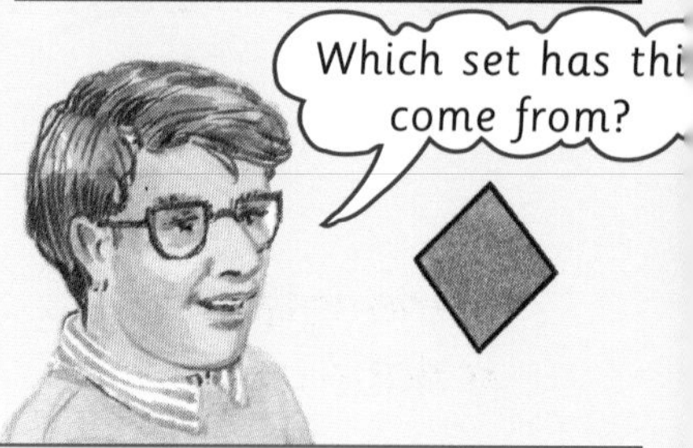

Which set has thi come from?

1 Copy and complete this table for sets A to E above.

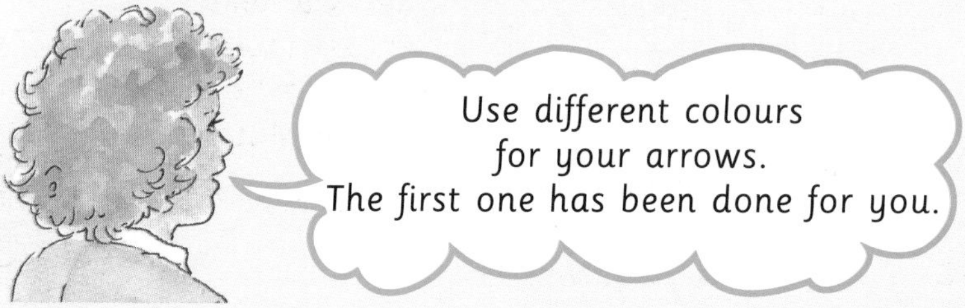

	belongs to the family of
A	hexagons
B	quadrilaterals
C	triangles
D	octagons
E	pentagons

Use different colours for your arrows. The first one has been done for you.

2 Write the family each of these shapes belongs to.

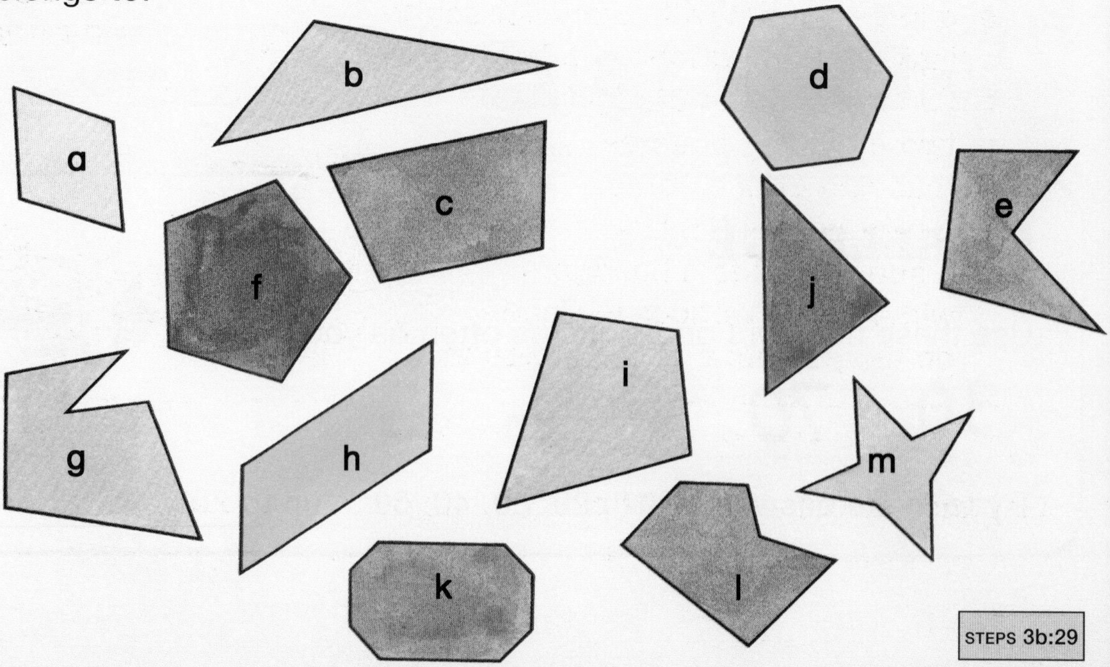

a b c d e f g h i j k l m

Shape challenges

6 x 6 geoboard, elastic bands, RM 62

Work with a partner if you can.

1 Write the letters **a** to **i** on the nine dotty grids on your copy of RM 62 .

2 Make on your geoboard, then record on your dotty grids, the shapes **a** to **i** listed below. Like this:

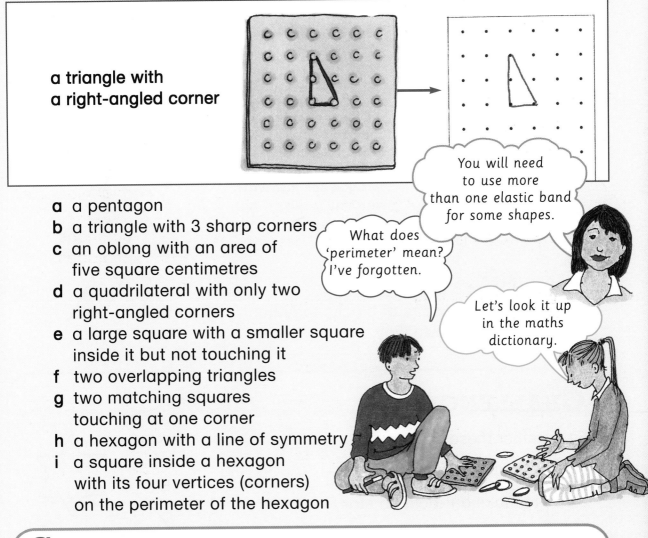

a triangle with a right-angled corner

You will need to use more than one elastic band for some shapes.

What does 'perimeter' mean? I've forgotten.

Let's look it up in the maths dictionary.

a a pentagon

b a triangle with 3 sharp corners

c an oblong with an area of five square centimetres

d a quadrilateral with only two right-angled corners

e a large square with a smaller square inside it but not touching it

f two overlapping triangles

g two matching squares touching at one corner

h a hexagon with a line of symmetry

i a square inside a hexagon with its four vertices (corners) on the perimeter of the hexagon

CHALLENGE

Get another copy of RM 62 and invent your own shape challenges.

New shapes from old

By fitting together pairs of Pattern Blocks in different ways, you can make new shapes.

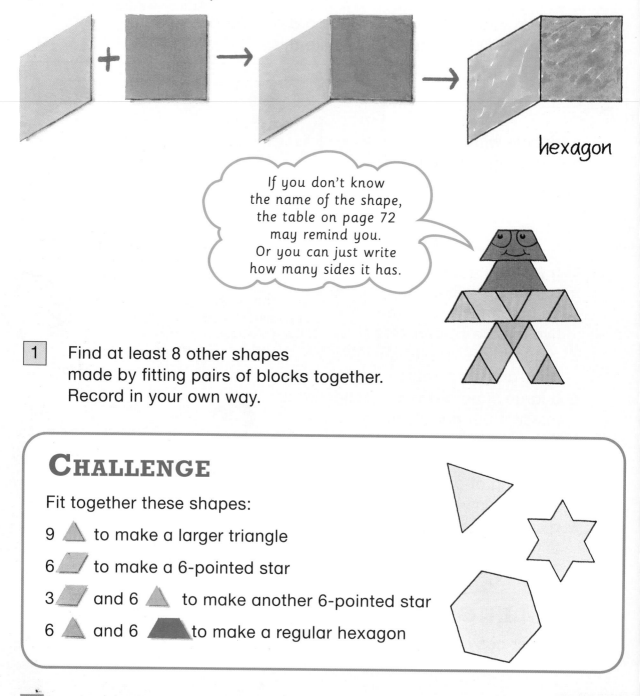

hexagon

If you don't know the name of the shape, the table on page 72 may remind you. Or you can just write how many sides it has.

1 Find at least 8 other shapes made by fitting pairs of blocks together. Record in your own way.

CHALLENGE

Fit together these shapes:

9 △ to make a larger triangle

6 ▱ to make a 6-pointed star

3 ▱ and 6 △ to make another 6-pointed star

6 △ and 6 ⬓ to make a regular hexagon

Make your own tile

card rectangles,
sticky tape, scissors,
backing sheet

1   Make a tessellating tile in this way.

- Cut a rectangle of card into two pieces
  from one corner to another like this.

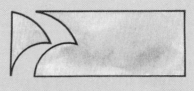

- Slide the cut-out piece to the opposite side
  and tape it in place.

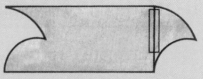

- Now cut out another piece from one side
  like this.

- Slide this piece to the opposite side
  and tape it in place anywhere along
  the top.

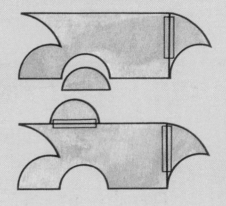

2   Try to make your new shape tessellate.

3   Decorate and colour at least part of your tessellation.

If you don't like the tile
you have made,
try again until
you get one you like.

Using scale ■ ■ ■ ■ ■ ■ ■ ■

1 Estimate how many centimetres long each was **before** it was drawn.

a

b

c

d

e

f

2 Now measure their length and ⟶ copy and complete this table.

3 Draw to one-fifth scale:

a a toy truck which is really 25 cm long.

b a stuffed toy snake which is really 40 cm long.

Drawing	One-fifth scale length	Real length
a		
b		
c		
d		
e		
f		

Plus and minus

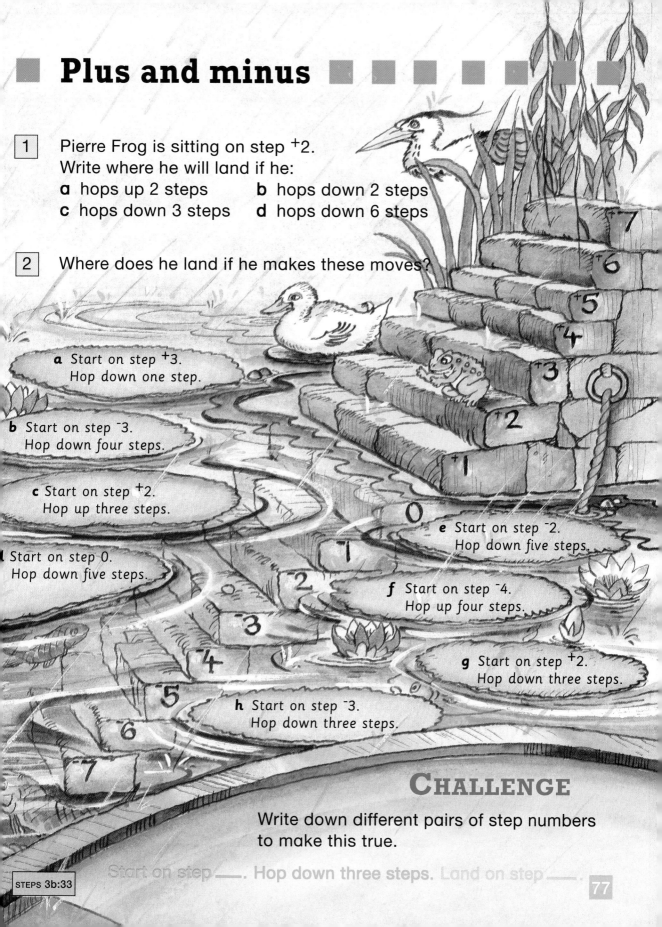

1 Pierre Frog is sitting on step $^+2$.
Write where he will land if he:
   a hops up 2 steps   **b** hops down 2 steps
   c hops down 3 steps   **d** hops down 6 steps

2 Where does he land if he makes these moves?

a Start on step $^+3$.
Hop down one step.

b Start on step $^-3$.
Hop down four steps.

c Start on step $^+2$.
Hop up three steps.

d Start on step 0.
Hop down five steps.

e Start on step $^-2$.
Hop down five steps.

f Start on step $^-4$.
Hop up four steps.

g Start on step $^+2$.
Hop down three steps.

h Start on step $^-3$.
Hop down three steps.

CHALLENGE

Write down different pairs of step numbers
to make this true.

Start on step ___. Hop down three steps. Land on step ___.

Temperatures

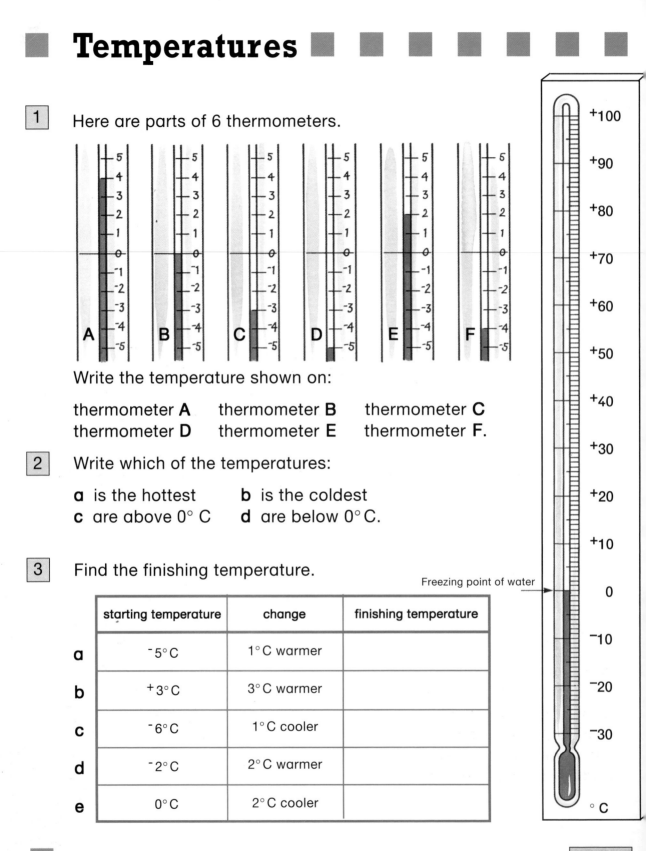

1   Here are parts of 6 thermometers.

Write the temperature shown on:

thermometer **A**   thermometer **B**   thermometer **C**
thermometer **D**   thermometer **E**   thermometer **F**.

2   Write which of the temperatures:

a is the hottest   **b** is the coldest
c are above 0° C   **d** are below 0°C.

3   Find the finishing temperature.

	starting temperature	change	finishing temperature
a	⁻5°C	1°C warmer	
b	⁺3°C	3°C warmer	
c	⁻6°C	1°C cooler	
d	⁻2°C	2°C warmer	
e	0°C	2°C cooler	

Freezing point of water

Mostly × and ÷ 3

Look carefully at Polly's 4-pointed star
to see how she used the numbers

Rules

- She had to put a **×** or **÷** sign at every corner.
- She had to put one **3** at every corner.

$12 \div 3 = 4$ $3 \times 4 = 12$

12

$4 \times 3 = 12$ $12 \div 4 = 3$

1   Make up more stars like Polly's with these numbers at the centre.

    a 24   **b** 15   **c** 27   **d** 21   **e** 30   **f** 18

2   Make up six **×** and **÷** stars using only these numbers.

    2   3   5   6   10   15   30   90

This number line shows how 2 × 7 and 7 × 2 are different.

$2 \times 7 = 14$

0 1 2 3 4 5 6 7 8 9 10 11 12 13 14

$7 \times 2 = 14$

3   Design number lines to show how these are different.

    a 3 × 7 and 7 × 3   **b** 9 × 3 and 3 × 9

CHALLENGE

Suzi bought nine monsters,
three at 18p each, three at 24p each
and three at 33p each.
Work out in your own way
what she paid for them
and her change from £5.

Mostly × and ÷ 4

1   Make five more 4-pointed stars like Polly's on page 79.

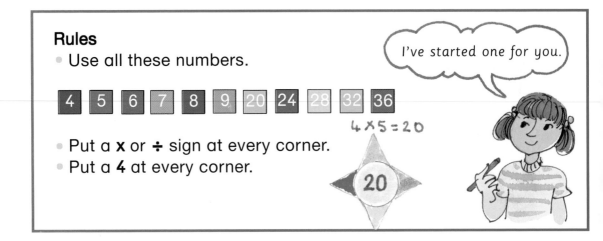

Rules
- Use all these numbers.

| 4 | 5 | 6 | 7 | 8 | 9 | 20 | 24 | 28 | 32 | 36 |

I've started one for you.

4×5=20

20

- Put a **×** or **÷** sign at every corner.
- Put a **4** at every corner.

2   Copy the arrow diagram and draw the missing arrows.

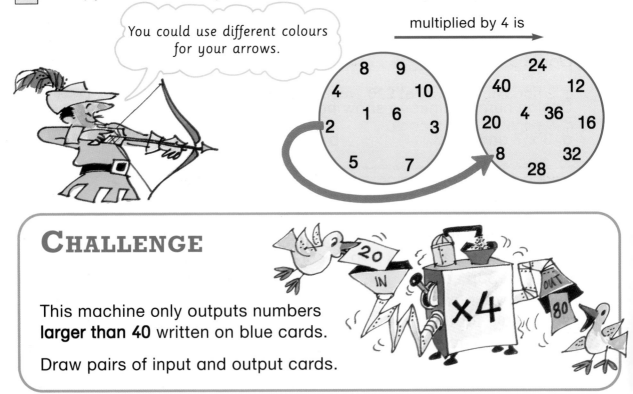

You could use different colours for your arrows.

multiplied by 4 is

8   9
4   10
1   6
2   3
5   7

24
40   12
20   4   36   16
8   32
28

CHALLENGE

20
IN
×4
OUT
80

This machine only outputs numbers **larger than 40** written on blue cards.

Draw pairs of input and output cards.

Garden centre

Decide the best way to find the answers to these.
Write down anything that helps.

1 Copy and complete the **purple** sentences.

    a 20 daffodils in a bunch. _____ daffodils in 4 bunches.
    140 daffodils make _____ bunches.

    b 30 snowdrop bulbs in a packet. _____ snowdrops in 6 packets.
    210 snowdrops bulbs in _____ packets.

    c 40 pansies in a tray. _____ pansies in 8 trays.
    240 pansies in _____ trays.

    d 50 garden canes in a bag. _____ canes in 7 bags.
    450 garden canes in _____ bags.

2 Work out the cost.

    a 2 hanging baskets at £20 each.   **b** 30 rose bushes at £5 each.

    c 4 gnomes at £40 each.   **d** 50 flower pots at £3 each.

3 Work out how much the garden centre will charge if someone buys
all the items in **2** .

CHALLENGE

Doug's mum wants to spend £90 on hanging baskets and roses.
Find different ways for her to spend her money.

Theme park

STEPS 3b:35

1 Write instructions to help someone go:

a from the **Entrance** to the **Water Ride**
b from the **Water Ride** to the **Café**
c from the **Café** to the **Water Ride**
d from the **Water Ride** to the **Entrance.**

2 Where will you end up if you do this?

a Start at the **Magic Castle**, walk N to the next attraction then walk NW.
b Start at the **Mirror Maze**, walk E to the next attraction and then walk SE.

3 Write two different routes for each journey

a **Ghost Train** to **Pirate Cave**   b **Rocket Ride** to **Mirror Maze**
c **Café** to **Computer Corner**   d **Water Ride** to **Helter Skelter**

4 Choose 5 attractions. Write instructions to travel from the **Entrance** to each one in turn and then to the **Exit**.

Try to choose the **shortest** route.

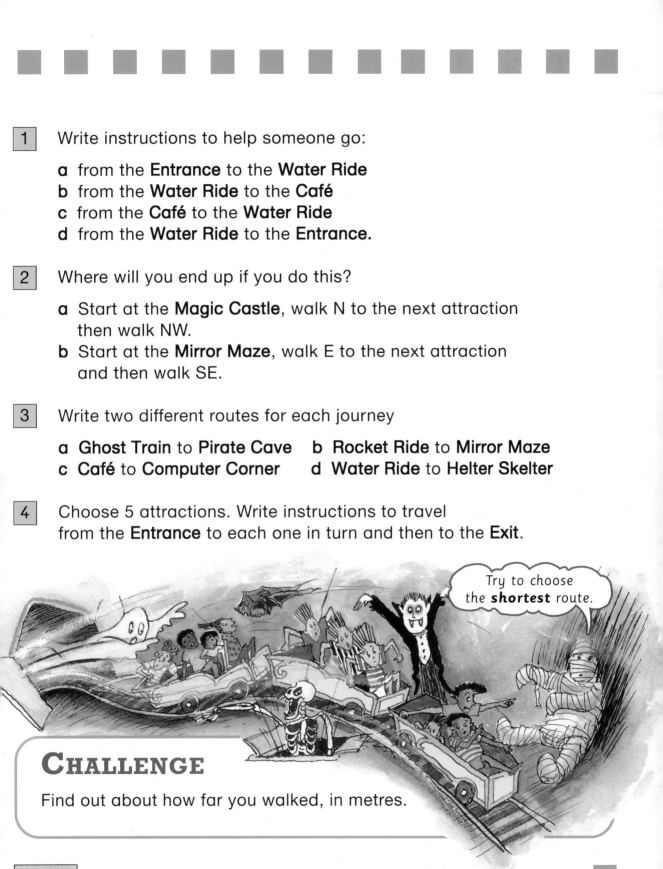

CHALLENGE

Find out about how far you walked, in metres.

Totals to 999

1 Copy and complete these sums. Use base 10 materials to help.

> *Remember to think: the answer will be about ...*

a 523 + 57 **b** 607 + 181 **c** 345 + 449
d 567 + 408 **e** 179 + 791 **f** 625 + 368

2 Write down which two sets added together make these totals.
Show how you work out your answers.

a 380 **b** 981 **c** 785
d 594 **e** 398 **f** 999

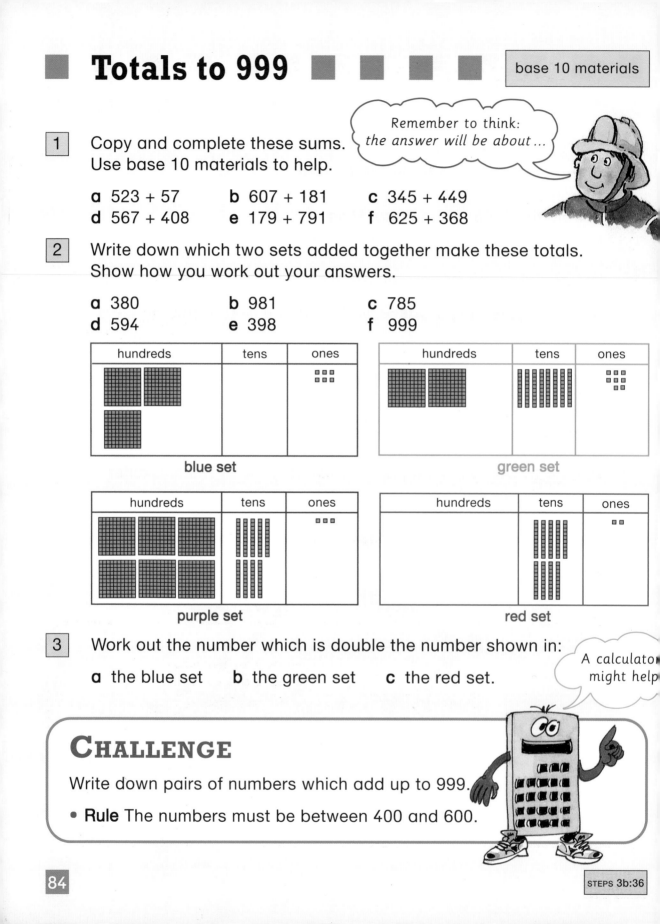

hundreds	tens	ones

blue set

hundreds	tens	ones

green set

hundreds	tens	ones

purple set

hundreds	tens	ones

red set

3 Work out the number which is double the number shown in:

> *A calculator might help*

a the blue set **b** the green set **c** the red set.

CHALLENGE

Write down pairs of numbers which add up to 999.

• **Rule** The numbers must be between 400 and 600.

Setting out sums ■ ■ ■ ■ ■ ■

Saria and Anil are learning to add without apparatus.

I like this way best.

I like this way best.

$$436 \longrightarrow 400 + 30 + 6$$
$$+ 123 \longrightarrow 100 + 20 + 3$$
$$500 + 50 + 9 \longrightarrow 559$$

```
  436
+ 123
    9  (6 + 3)
   50  (30 + 20)
  500  (400 + 100)
  559
```

1 Use Saria's way to find the totals.

a 136 + 432 **b** 247 + 631 **c** 527 + 71
d 805 + 164 **e** 43 + 710 **f** 910 + 89

2 Now use Anil's way to find the totals
for the sums in **1**.

3 Use your favourite way to find the answers to these.

a 128 + 301 **b** 346 + 420 **c** 547 + 58
d 717 + 77 **e** 874 + 86 **f** 358 + 609

CHALLENGE

Find at least five ways to make this correct.

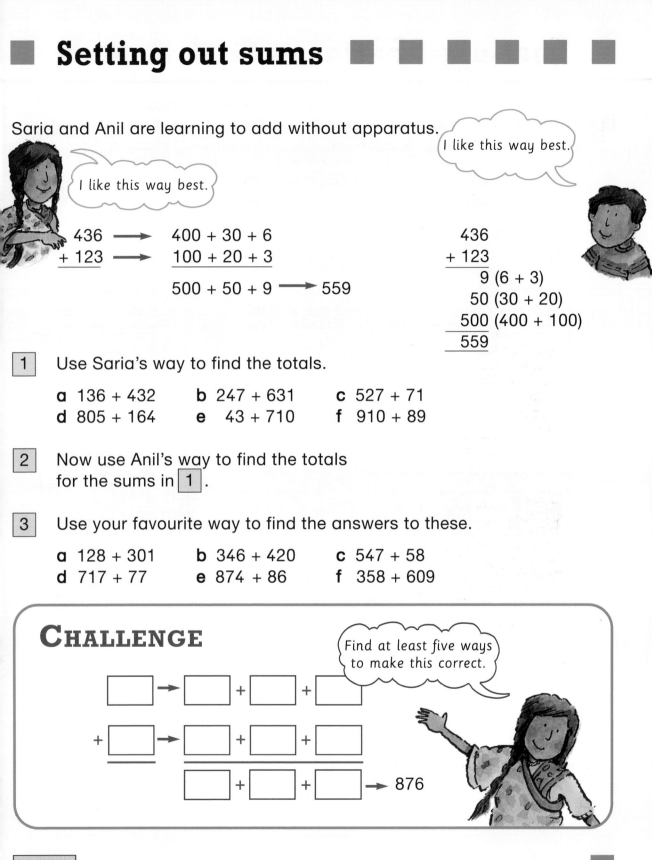

□ ⟶ □ + □ + □
+ □ ⟶ □ + □ + □
□ + □ + □ ⟶ 876

Last-digit patterns

1 Write the sequence of **last digits** in the colours shown for:

a the two-times table

b the one-times table.

Two-times table

1 x 2 = 2
2 x 2 = 4
3 x 2 = 6
4 x 2 = 8
5 x 2 = 10
6 x 2 = 12
7 x 2 = 14
8 x 2 = 16
9 x 2 = 18
10 x 2 = 20

One-times table

1 x 1 = 1
2 x 1 = 2
3 x 1 = 3
4 x 1 = 4
5 x 1 = 5
6 x 1 = 6
7 x 1 = 7
8 x 1 = 8
9 x 1 = 9
10 x 1 = 10

2 a Write the three-times, four-times and five-times tables.

b Colour the last digits using this code.

> If you don't have the right colours, you can make your own colour code.

0 yellow	1 pink	2 red	3 light blue	4 dark green
5 purple	6 brown	7 black	8 dark blue	9 light green

3 Work out times-tables to match these chains of colour.

a

b

CHALLENGE

Which other times-tables match these chains?

a   b

Digital sums

■ 1 Ben made a number and colour pattern.
He **added the digits** in the answers in the three-times table.

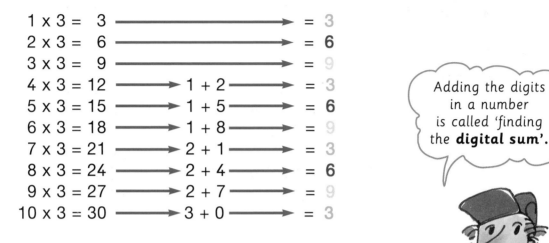

1 x 3 = 3 ——————————————→ = 3
2 x 3 = 6 ——————————————→ = 6
3 x 3 = 9 ——————————————→ = 9
4 x 3 = 12 ——————→ 1 + 2 ——————→ = 3
5 x 3 = 15 ——————→ 1 + 5 ——————→ = 6
6 x 3 = 18 ——————→ 1 + 8 ——————→ = 9
7 x 3 = 21 ——————→ 2 + 1 ——————→ = 3
8 x 3 = 24 ——————→ 2 + 4 ——————→ = 6
9 x 3 = 27 ——————→ 2 + 7 ——————→ = 9
10 x 3 = 30 ——————→ 3 + 0 ——————→ = 3

Adding the digits in a number is called 'finding the **digital sum**'.

a Write the two-times table.
b Calculate and colour the **digital sums** as Ben did.

Use the colour code on page 86 (opposite).

■ 2 Which times-tables match these chains
of colours of **digital sums**?

a

b

CHALLENGE

Which other times-table has digital sums which match this chain?

▲ ▲ ▲ ▲ ▲ ▲ ▲ ▲ ▲ ▲

Dragon cards ■ ■ ■ ■ ■ ■

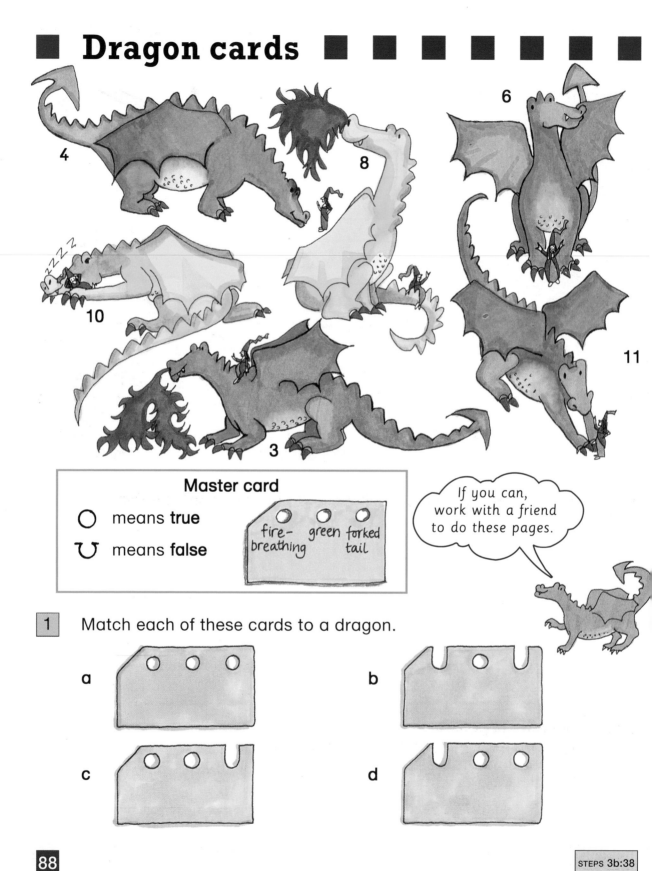

Master card

○ means **true**

ʊ means **false**

fire-breathing · green · forked tail

If you can, work with a friend to do these pages.

1 Match each of these cards to a dragon.

a

b

c

d

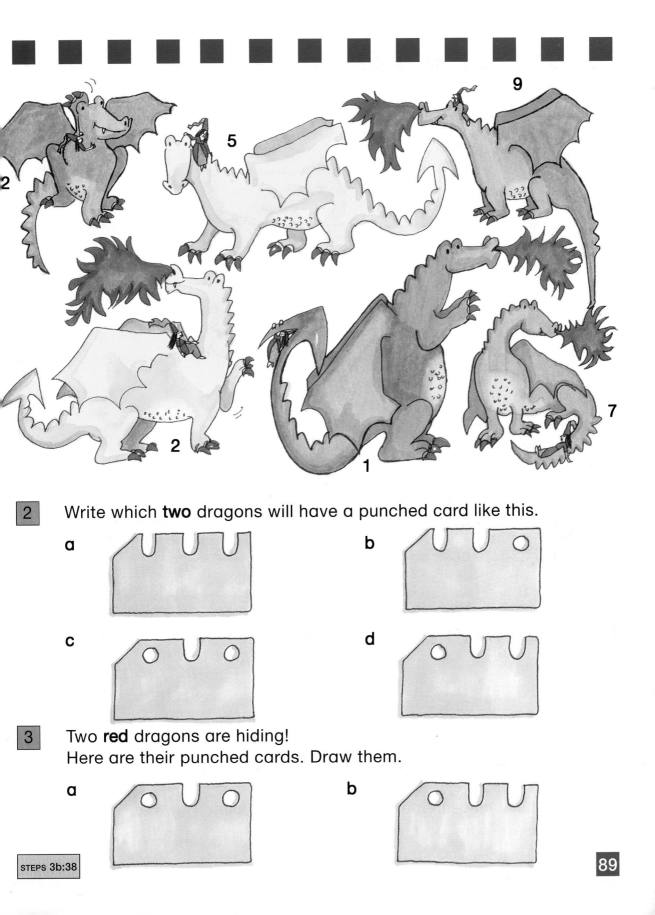

2 Write which **two** dragons will have a punched card like this.

a

b

c

d

3 Two **red** dragons are hiding!
Here are their punched cards. Draw them.

a

b

Group survey

The children in a group in Mr Perry's class have been measuring their heights to the nearest centimetre, and weights to the nearest kilogram. Here are their measurements.

1   Use these measurements to help you complete RM 139.

Back to the start

Work with a friend if you can.

Zelma and Clare had to decide how to get back to the block they started with. They had to put blocks in between which made **one change at a time**.

Here are two of the ways they found.

1. START

red to blue small to large blue to red large to small

2. start

circle to triangle small to large yellow to red triangle to circle large to small red to yellow

3. START

1 Use different blocks. For each, make one change at a time to get back to the start. Record what you do.

One change only

Tim changed a small, blue, thin triangular block into a large, red, thick, circular block.

Then he drew this diagram to show what he did.

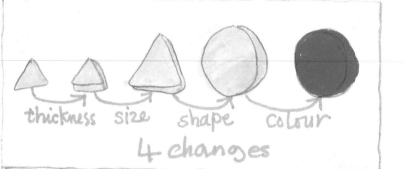

Tess did the same but she did it like this!

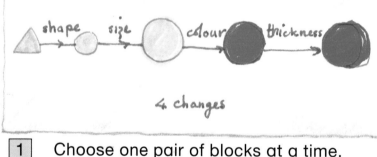

Rule
Make only **one** change at a time.

Remember the rule!

| 1 | Choose one pair of blocks at a time. |

| 2 | In your own way, write down how you change one block into the other. |

CHALLENGE

Choose two blocks.
Find and write down different ways of changing one into the other.